PADI DIVE MANUAL

P·A·D·I

INTERNATIONAL

PADI DIVE

Written by Dennis Graver

Reviewed by PADI Master Instructor Review Committee

Design, layout, and production by Paul Hill, Anne Okimoto

Illustrated by Jim Mitchell, Paul Hill, Anne Okimoto

Photography by Dennis Graver, Paul Hill,
Paul Tzimoulis, John Lidington

Photography model: Verlee King

Cover photo by Chuck Nicklin - The Diving Locker

Consultants: PADI Board of Directors, PADI Executive
Committee, PADI Advisory Board, major diving
equipment manufacturers, Skin Diver Magazine

Typography by Ken Hortness Graphics
and Type Incorporated

Printed by Orange County Lithograph Co.

Published by Professional Association of Diving Instructors

Published by the Professional Association of Diving Instructors,
2064 North Bush Street, Santa Ana, CA 92706

Printed in the United States of America

CONTENTS

SECTION 1

- **Introduction**
- **Adapting to the Underwater World**
- **Skin Diving Equipment**
- **Respiration**
- **Using Skin Diving Equipment**
- **Skin Diving Skills**

Introduction

Welcome to the course! Congratulations on your decision to pursue the excitement and adventure of diving. You are about to learn the knowledge, skills, and habits which will allow you to safely explore innerspace — the other three quarters of our planet where fantastic beauty awaits and an infinite variety of interesting life abounds. Within the wonderful liquid environment of the world's water you'll discover countless things to capture your interest and stimulate your imagination.

The knowledge and ability gained from this course will provide a vehicle for visiting the fantastic underwater world. There are numerous underwater activities to be pursued for gratification, some of which are quite technical and require additional training. This course and your Instructor will prepare you to engage in basic diving activities in your local area at shallow

depths and under calm conditions. For diving in other regions or under different conditions, additional training and orientation are essential.

It is difficult for the non-diver to perceive the underwater world. It seems mysterious and somewhat hostile. As diving experience is gained, however, the mystery is reduced, and the hostility fades and is replaced with curiosity, awe, and respect. It is difficult to imagine remaining submerged for prolonged periods in an alien environment where pressure presses in on every side, yet we live submerged . . . submerged in a sea of air, and the effects of going under water are only changed by the greater weight of the liquid. When we can cope with this increased weight, which is pressure, and can take an air supply with us, we can adapt very well to submerging ourselves in water also. With proper equipment, knowledge, and skills we may enter the water in complete

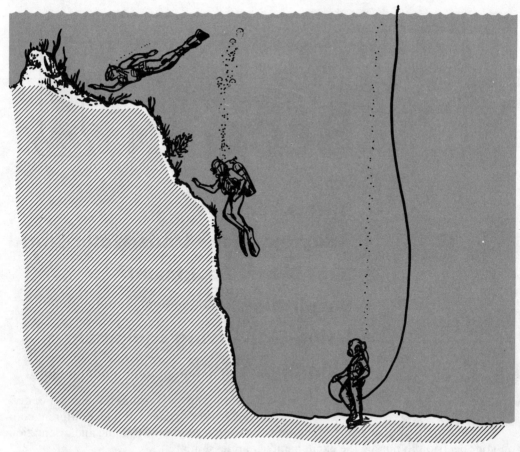

Various forms of diving - skin diving, scuba diving, and surface-supplied diving

safety and with no discomfort whatsoever. We can explore there with mask, snorkel, and fins while holding our breath as a skin diver (also called a "Free Diver"), or can prolong our visit with the use of scuba (Self-Contained Underwater Breathing Apparatus) equipment. Other methods of diving, such as surface-supplied or commercial diving, are beyond the scope of recreational diving and require extensive specialized training.

The prerequisites for participation in a scuba course are easily met by most individuals. You should be reasonably healthy and have a good circulation and respiration. Physically, you should be a reasonably proficient swimmer and be comfortable and relaxed in the water. Mentally, you should have a mature attitude, good judgment, and self-discipline.

Completion of this course is only the beginning of your education in diving. Much will be learned through personal experience afterwards, but additional skills to expand your diving capabilities and increase your enjoyment can be obtained through Advanced Diver courses, Divemaster training, and diving Specialty courses. There are many things to do as a diver, and learning how to do them the correct way through proper training makes them easier and more enjoyable. Plan now to obtain additional training to expand your diving capabilities.

The Complete Training Program

At PADI, the emphasis is on increased training in actual diving conditions. At the heart of the PADI training concept is the five dive Open Water Certification Course, a step-by-step method of instruction that eases you into the proper skills to pursue your interest in the sport of scuba diving.

PADI offers a complete curriculum for a variety of achievement levels beyond Open Water Diver - such as Advanced Open Water Diver and Master Scuba Diver.

In addition, PADI offers ten specialty courses. With this self-motivating curriculum, you can progress as far as you desire and at your own rate. At each achievement level, you receive more knowledge of the water world and discover different ways to have fun in the water.

SKIN DIVER

BASIC SCUBA DIVER

OPEN WATER DIVER

ADVANCED OPEN WATER DIVER

DIVEMASTER

ASSISTANT INSTRUCTOR

UNDERWATER INSTRUCTOR

OPEN WATER INSTRUCTOR

SPECIALTY INSTRUCTOR

MASTER INSTRUCTOR

MASTER SCUBA DIVER
(Any Five of Ten Specialties)

Search and Recovery Diver	Ice Diver
Underwater Photographer	Deep Diver
Equipment Specialist	Wreck Diver
Underwater Hunter	Cavern Diver
Research Diver	Rescue Diver

PADI Positive Identification Certification card, commonly referred to as a "C-Card"

CERTIFICATION

Upon successful completion of this course, you will be awarded a PADI certification card. This credential attests to your completion of training and ability to meet standard requirements established by the Professional Association of Diving Instructors. Retailers, boat operators, and others in diving everywhere will ask to see your "C-card" as evidence of your training. Your diving credential will be required to obtain compressed air, rent or purchase equipment, and participate in diving activities.

The Professional Association of Diving Instructors (PADI) establishes the standards for diver training, trains and certifies Instructors who teach people to dive, provides support services and materials to members, and maintains records of training activities. PADI is the largest diver training agency in the world, with the most complete program of diver education. The safety record of PADI is outstanding and reflects the ability of its professional members. As you earn each PADI certification, you can be proud, for you are earning the finest and most respected credentials available.

COURSE OVERVIEW

The training program is divided into three major sections: (1) Knowledge; (2) Skill Development; and (3) Open Water Application. For each academic session there is a text and study guide section, as well as a minimum standards quiz which needs to be completed with a satisfactory score before progressing to the next academic level. For each Skill Development session there are specific objectives and a skill proficiency drill which needs to be satisfactorily completed before participating in the next level of skill development. Sessions may be repeated as needed. PADI has structured the course in this manner so students may progress according to individual ability, and student preparedness is assured for the learning of more complex knowledge and skills. Open Water Application is structured to provide an orientation to diving in the local environment, where knowledge and skills learned are applied to actual diving situations.

You may enroll in either the Open Water Scuba Diver course (recommended) or the Basic Scuba Diver course. The Open Water Scuba Diver course, which prepares the diver to make repetitive dives to depths

The three major areas of diver training are: classroom, pool or sheltered water, and open water.

of approximately 60 feet and includes basic navigation, consists of five academic sessions, five skills development sessions, an open water skin dive, and four open water scuba dives. The Basic Scuba Diver course, providing fundamentals for limited underwater excursions to approximately 30 feet, does not include nagivation, has less academics than the Open Water Diver course, and has only three open water training dives.

This text will clearly outline the knowledge and skills you'll need for completion of training. It's up to you, with your Instructor's assistance, to achieve these objectives. Your Instructor is a highly trained professional, able and willing to help you develop into a capable diver. Ask questions and expect individual attention. It is your Instructor's goal to help you fulfill your desire to become a diver.

Within each topic area in the text are skill and knowledge goals for you to achieve. These goals are identified in boxes at the beginning of each topic, and state precisely what you'll need to know and be able to do to successfully complete each training module. Study these goals carefully, so you can focus your attention toward them during instruction. Here is an example of course goals:

GOALS

In order to learn to dive, you should be capable of performing the following waterskills without swimming aids. You will be required to demonstrate them at the first session.

1. Swim 200 yards nonstop using two or more strokes. Form and comfort are more important than speed.
2. Swim at least 40 feet underwater on a single breath of air.
3. Dive to a depth of 8 to 10 feet, recover a five pound object, and swim the object to the surface.
4. Tread water for at least five minutes.
5. Float, drownproof, or bob with a minimum amount of movement for at least five minutes.

These skills are not difficult, and are minimum prerequisites.

Note: Units of measurement are expressed in U.S. increments through this book. A table for conversion to metric units is included in the appendix.

Adapting to the Underwater World

We live in a gaseous environment, but seldom consider how we see, hear and move in air, because we are adapted to it — it is normal to us. Water is nearly 900 times as dense as air, and when we change the density of the medium surrounding us, we find the effects on light, sound, heat, and motion different from those of air. To participate in diving, we need to understand these effects and learn how we can adapt to a liquid environment.

GOALS

By the end of this module, you should be able to explain differences in vision, hearing, heat loss, body movements, and weight in water as compared to air.

UNDERWATER VISION

To see clearly underwater, an air space is needed in front of the eyes. Without an air space the rays of light entering the eye cannot be focused properly and blurred vision results. You can still see, although not clearly, and this blurred vision is useful to you to distinguish gross objects. When an air space is maintained for the eye to see through, as when a mask is used, everything is clearly in focus. However, objects are magnified by the water approximately 25%, causing them to appear larger and closer.

Magnification of objects by water

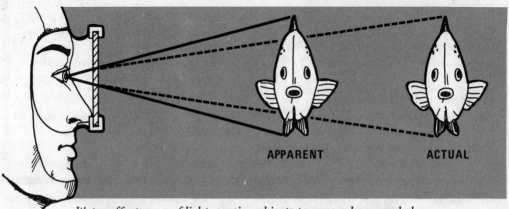

APPARENT   ACTUAL

Water affects rays of light, causing objects to appear larger and closer.

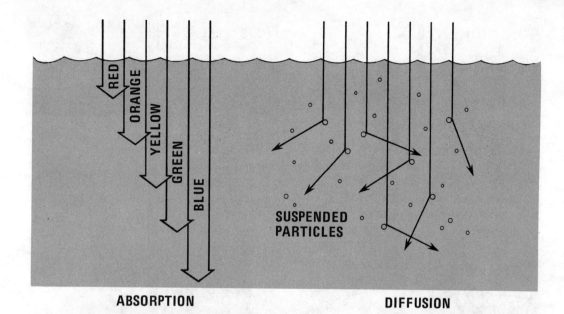

ABSORPTION   DIFFUSION

Absorption and diffusion of light rays in water

Water has other effects on light. As you descend, there is less light. This is due to several factors. Some of the light is scattered by particles suspended in the water, and some of it is absorbed by the water itself. White light, such as sunlight, is composed of various colors, which are absorbed in water one by one as depth increases. Each color is a part of the total light entering the water, and as each color is absorbed, less light remains to penetrate further. Reds and yellows are absorbed first, with blue reaching the greatest depth. You may not see many beautiful colors underwater because the light needed to display the colors cannot reach their depth. However, an underwater light at close range will reveal true colors.

UNDERWATER HEARING

The underwater world is definitely not a quiet place. You'll hear many new and interesting sounds there. Sound travels very well in water, but it is difficult to determine the direction from which a sound is coming. It is extremely difficult to get sound into water from air, so speech underwater without the assistance of special equipment is almost totally ineffective. Sound underwater is typically used only to gain the attention of another diver.

HEAT LOSS IN WATER

In air, body heat is lost as it rises from the skin into the air, is carried away by air currents, or through cooling by evaporation of perspiration. In water, body heat is lost much faster than in air. The loss of body heat in water can lead to a serious condition in a short period of time unless insulation is provided to reduce heat loss. Because water has such a great capacity for heat, even seemingly warm water can cause chilling. Insulation with an exposure suit is recommended for diving in water 75° F or colder. Shivering is a symptom that heat loss has reached a critical level. When you begin shivering uncontrollably, get out of the water immediately and seek warmth.

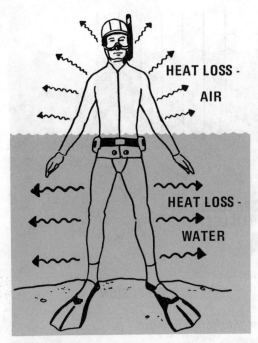

Body heat loss in water

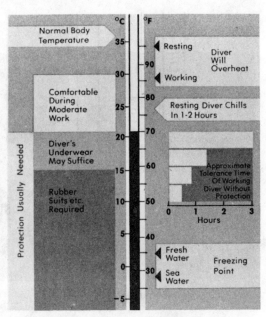

Effects of water temperature

MOTION IN WATER

Due to the greater density of water, resistance to body movement is much greater in water than in air. Because of this, it is necessary to make slow and deliberate movements in water. Rapid, jerky movements waste energy needlessly. When swimming or moving underwater, move slowly and steadily for efficiency. For propulsion through water, divers wear fins to allow the large, powerful leg muscles to push the larger surface area of the fins against the water.

The amount of surface area exposed when moving through water affects the amount of physical energy required for propulsion. A streamlined object presenting a small frontal area will require less energy to move at the same speed as an object with a large and rough frontal area. Streamline yourself for diving and swim horizontally, so less work will be required to move through the water.

Trying to swim fast or work hard in water as a diver causes exhaustion quickly. Learn to pace yourself, take it easy, and relax in water. These are important aspects of your diver training.

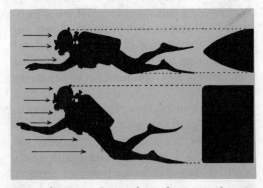

Streamlining reduces frontal area and resistance to movement in water.

WEIGHT IN WATER

Have you ever noticed how light you feel when standing in water? Isn't it difficult to get traction to walk or run? That's because

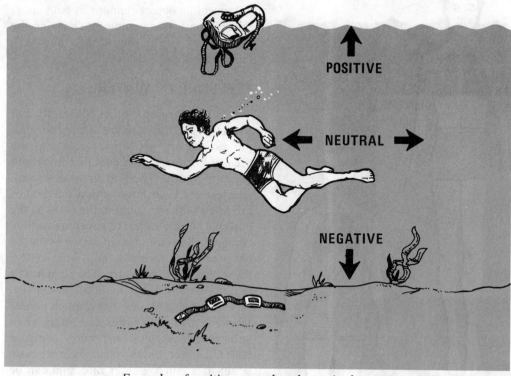

Examples of positive, neutral, and negative buoyancy.

an object weighs less in water than in air. If an object displaces an amount of water weighing more than its own weight, it will float. If the amount of water displaced weighs less than the weight of the object, the object will sink, and if the object displaces water equal to its own weight, the object will neither float nor sink, but will remain suspended at any depth. If an object floats, it is said to be positively buoyant; if it sinks, it is negatively buoyant; and if it neither floats nor sinks, it is neutrally buoyant.

Through proper control of buoyancy, with weights and buoyancy control device, a diver can be positively buoyant at the surface in order to conserve energy; and can be neutrally buoyant underwater, weightless and able to move freely in all directions. Control of buoyancy is one of the most important skills for a diver to master. When this can be done easily, a great deal of energy can be conserved. Adapting to this effect of water is not difficult, and can be learned easily through instruction and practice.

The amount of buoyancy provided by a liquid depends on the weight of the liquid. Salt water weighs more than fresh water for a given volume, due to dissolved salts. Therefore, an object or a diver will be more buoyant in salt water than in fresh water.

Most people are positively buoyant in water. In fact, when floating motionless at the surface, most divers need to exhale air from their lungs in order to sink. By exhaling, the lungs are decreased in volume, less water is displaced, and less buoyancy results. We can see then, that changing the volume of an object changes its buoyancy. Divers control buoyancy by changing the volume of air in their lungs and in a buoyancy control device.

PRESSURE IN WATER

Air exerts pressure on us constantly, but we do not feel the pressure. This is because our bodies are primarily liquid and the pressure is distributed equally throughout the entire body. The few air spaces (ears, sinuses, etc.) we have within our bodies are filled with air equal in pressure to the external air pressure. However, as altitude changes, the amount of air above us (or the air pressure), changes; and we can feel these changes in pressure. They can be felt in our ears when driving in the mountains or when flying. Water, being much denser than air, also exerts pressure on us when submerged. As with air, water pressure isn't felt either, but the changes in pressure occur at a much greater rate, and can be felt. What we feel is a difference in pressure between the external pressure and the

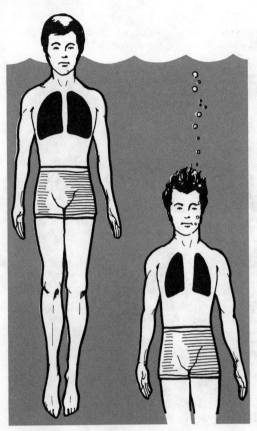

Effect of lung volume on buoyancy

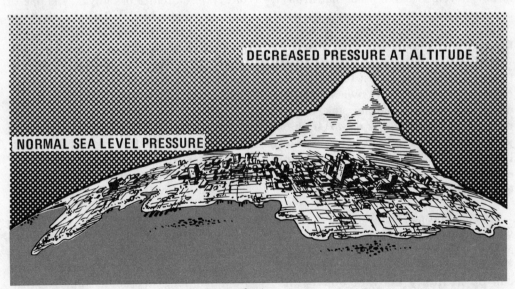

DECREASED PRESSURE AT ALTITUDE

NORMAL SEA LEVEL PRESSURE

Atmospheric pressure

pressure in our body air spaces. As long as these pressures are equal, there is no sensation. When water pressure increases with depth, it presses inward on air spaces, causing discomfort unless air pressure can be increased inside the air space, such as in the ears or sinuses. By increasing the air pressure in an air space to equal external pressure, the pressures are equalized and discomfort due to pressure changes can be completely avoided. By equalizing pressures in air spaces as we change depth, the mechanical effects of changing pressure will have no more effect on us than air pressure does at the surface. There are various air spaces we need to equalize when diving, and you will learn these equalizing techniques through training and experience.

As you descend, you will feel the effects of pressure on your mask and in your ears even in shallow water. Equalize these pressures by exhaling slightly into your mask and then blocking the nostrils while attempting to exhale through the nose to add air to the air spaces inside the ears.

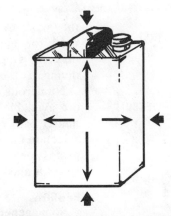

EQUALIZED AT NORMAL PRESSURE

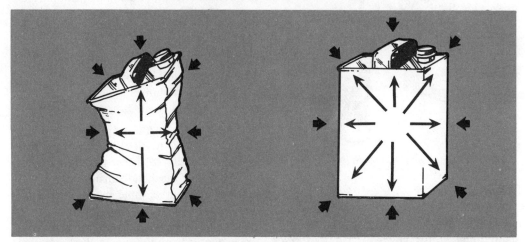

UNEQUALIZED AT INCREASED PRESSURE   **EQUALIZED AT INCREASED PRESSURE**

Effects of pressure

Skin Diving Equipment

In order to adapt ourselves to a liquid environment, certain items of equipment are needed. We have seen how the effects of water create a need for: (1) an air space in front of the eyes, (2) some form of insulation for the body, and (3) a means of controlling buoyancy. Equipment exists which allows us to deal with various effects of water and to dive beneath its surface.

GOALS

By the end of this module, you should be able to explain the purpose, function, selection criteria, preparation for use, and care and maintenance **OF** mask, snorkel, fins, buoyancy control device, exposure suit, weight belt, knife, and gear bag

AND

to explain the cause, prevention, and first aid for cramps

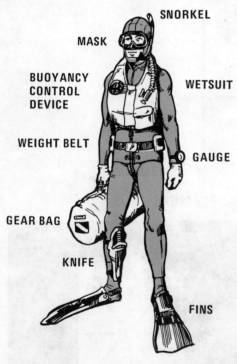

Equipment for skin diving

SNORKEL

MASK

BUOYANCY CONTROL DEVICE

WETSUIT

WEIGHT BELT

GAUGE

GEAR BAG

KNIFE

FINS

MASK

As previously mentioned, the mask allows a person to see clearly underwater by maintaining an air space in front of the eyes. This air space is subject to the effects of water pressure, and must be equalized underwater, so the nose is included inside the mask to permit exhalation into the mask for equalization of pressure during descent. Goggles are not acceptable for diving, as they cannot be equalized.

Numerous styles and shapes of masks are available, and the type selected is a matter of personal preference after other selection factors have been considered. A professional diving retailer will help you select a mask best suited to your needs.

Features

Some generally desirable mask features are noted in the illustration. Additional features worthy of consideration include:

1. A means to seal the nostrils from outside the mask
2. A purge valve (optional)
3. A wide field of vision
4. Low volume
5. Visual correction (as needed)

Finger wells or a nose pocket allow access to the nose to block the nostrils. This is done to equalize air pressure in internal air spaces in the head during descent. A mask should have some means to permit equalization easily.

A purge valve is a one-way valve used to expel water from the mask. With practice it is easy to clear the water from a mask without a purge valve, so the valve is an optional feature.

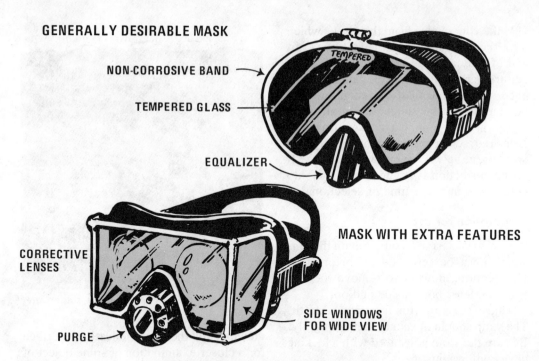

GENERALLY DESIRABLE MASK

NON-CORROSIVE BAND

TEMPERED GLASS

EQUALIZER

MASK WITH EXTRA FEATURES

CORRECTIVE LENSES

PURGE

SIDE WINDOWS FOR WIDE VIEW

Diving masks with various features

Wide view masks provide a greater field of vision and simply allow you to see more while diving. A wider field of view is achieved by various methods, such as placing the lens close to the eyes, or including side windows in masks.

Low volume masks require less air to equalize or clear of water, and are more of a concern to a skin diver, with limited air, than to a scuba diver, who has a source of air available underwater.

Visual correction in masks is available with several methods from which to choose.

Selection

The most important factors in the selection of basic equipment are fit and comfort. This is particularly true of a mask. It must fit precisely. To test fit, place the mask against the face very gently without the strap in place and inhale through the nose. A properly fitting mask should pull into place due to the suction created by breath-

ing air out of the mask and should stay in place as long as you continue to inhale. If you must push the mask onto your face to get this result, the fit is not proper, and other masks should be tested until a perfect fit is achieved. Next, be sure you can seal your nostrils easily from outside the mask.

Testing mask fit. You should be able to "sniff" the mask into place if it fits properly.

Make your choice from the masks which have the generally desirable features of fit and of easy access to the nose. All other features are a matter of personal preference, but a wide field of vision and low volume should be sought when all other factors are the same. If a mask with a purge is desired, select one with a larger purge, as small purge valves are rather ineffective. If visual correction is needed, take this into consideration at the time of selection.

Preparation for use

New masks have an oily film on the lens which must be scrubbed off before use. Use scouring powder to remove the film from the lens, both inside and out.

Adjust the strap for a comfortable fit. The strap should fit snugly, but not tightly. Be sure the strap is secured with a locking device after adjustment.

SNORKEL

The snorkel allows a diver to breathe without lifting the head out of the water while at the surface. With proper buoyancy adjustment, a diver can lie motionless at the surface and breathe through the snorkel with uninterrupted underwater

The snorkel allows continuous underwater viewing

viewing, and then dive beneath the surface for a closer examination of some object of interest. The snorkel is also used for breathing at the surface to conserve scuba air for underwater use. It is a very simple device, being little more than a J-shaped tube which fits comfortably in the mouth and extends above the surface.

There are several types of snorkels available. Your diving retailer will assist you in selecting the snorkel best suited to your physique and application.

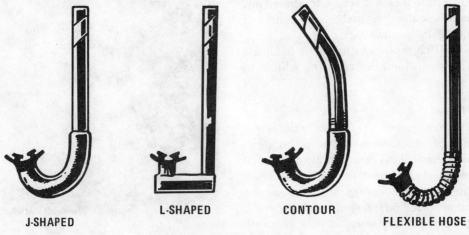

J-SHAPED   **L-SHAPED**   **CONTOUR**   **FLEXIBLE HOSE**

Various types of snorkels

Features

The most important feature of a snorkel is its breathing ease. You do not want a snorkel which restricts breathing severely. Bore diameter, length, and bends all affect breathing resistance. Avoid long, skinny snorkels. An acceptable snorkel will have at least a ¾ inch diameter bore and be about 12-14 inches in length.

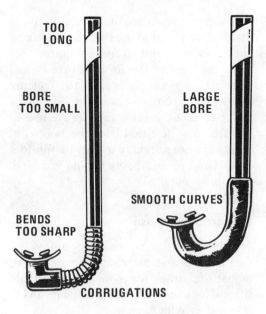

Factors affecting breathing ease

As you will discover, water entering a snorkel can be cleared simply, so a means to prevent water from entering is not required. In fact, it is important that the snorkel *not* have any such device, as it will reduce the ease of breathing.

Selection

The important considerations are comfort, fit, and minimum breathing resistance. To check these factors, place the snorkel in your mouth with the mouthpiece flange between your lips and teeth, and the barrel of the snorkel against the front of your left ear. The mouthpiece should be comfortable and straight in your mouth.

Next, breathe hard through the snorkel to test ease of breathing. Try various snorkels to compare comfort and breathing ease.

Preparation for use

Attach the snorkel to your mask strap on the left side with the small rubber snorkel keeper provided with the snorkel. As in the illustration, one loop of the keeper goes

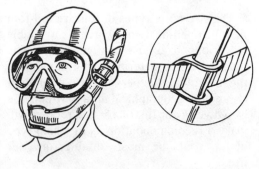

Snorkel-to-mask attachment

around the snorkel, the straight part between the keeper loops goes around the mask strap, and the other keeper loop then goes onto the snorkel. The keeper is then worked down on the snorkel to the approximate height needed to reach the mouth with the mask in place.

Next, don the mask and position the snorkel near the front of your left ear, then adjust the snorkel height and rotation until the snorkel remains in the mouth even when the mouth is opened widely. The muscles of the mouth should not be required to hold the snorkel in position when properly adjusted.

FINS

Hand and arm movements are ineffective for underwater propulsion, when compared to swimming with fins, which provide a large surface to be driven by powerful leg muscles. Fins provide more powerful propulsion than arms and free the hands for other activities.

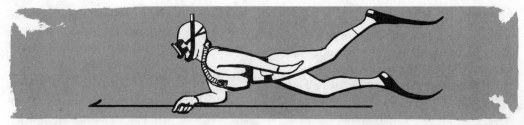

Fins provide a means of easy propulsion and allow the hands to be used for other purposes besides swimming.

The two basic types of fins are full-foot fins and open-heel fins, which are available in various sizes and configurations. The type needed is determined by the size of the individual, the person's physical ability, and the geographical area in which one is to dive. Your Instructor and retailer will make a recommendation as to which type of fin would be most suitable for your needs.

Features and Selection

The various features of fins are unimportant compared to blade size and rigidity.

The larger and stiffer the blade, the more strength required to use the fin. Determine the type, size, and stiffness requirements first, then select the fin based on fit and comfort. If boots to protect the feet are commonly worn in the area, they should be purchased at the same time as the fins so the fins can be fitted with the boots on. Boots are not normally worn with full-foot fins. The fins and boots should not bind, cramp, or pinch.

Preparation for use

No preparation is necessary unless the fins have adjustable straps. In this case, adjust the straps for a snug, comfortable fit, and lock them in place if some means to do so is provided.

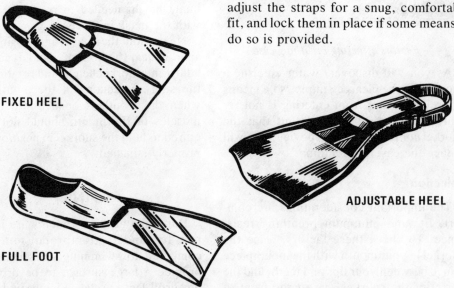

FIXED HEEL

FULL FOOT

ADJUSTABLE HEEL

Types of swim fins

Obtain professional advice when selecting fins

Cramps

A cramp is a painful involuntary muscle contraction, usually occurring in the leg or foot of a diver and caused by working the muscle too hard, restricted circulation, or cold. Fins can contribute to cramping if they are too large and stiff for the diver or if the diver works too hard when using them. With fitness, proper selection of fins, conditioning in the use of fins, proper insulation, and pacing of activity, cramping of muscles can be avoided.

Should a cramp occur while diving, stretch the cramped muscle and massage it to increase circulation. A good method to stretch a cramped calf muscle is to pull upwards on the tip of the fin. After the cramp is removed, rest the muscle before continuing at a slower pace.

Cramp release

Various Buoyancy Control Devices

BUOYANCY CONTROL DEVICE

A Buoyancy Control Device (BCD) for diving is an inflatable bladder, which can be orally or mechanically inflated with gas to increase buoyancy, and which also has a means to exhaust the gas. It is a mandatory piece of equipment for all diving and is used to provide surface support for resting, swimming, or assistance, and to maintain neutral buoyancy underwater. A diver picking up objects which are heavy and cause negative buoyancy can add air to the BCD, increasing its volume and buoyancy, and achieve neutral buoyancy to reduce the effort needed to move about underwater with the heavy objects.

Many styles and types of BCD's are available, some of which are quite sophisticated and require special training in their use. A discussion with your Instructor, re-tailer, and local divers of the advantages and disadvantages of the various Buoyancy Control Devices available will help in deciding which type is appropriate for your physical size and geographical diving area.

Desirable Features

An acceptable BCD will have a large diameter inflation/deflation hose mounted at or near the top of the bladder for ease in expelling air. An essential feature is a pressure relief valve to prevent rupture of the device from overexpansion. The configuration and harness of the unit should be comfortable and designed to keep the device from riding up around the diver's neck when inflated. Controls should be easy to locate, distinguish, and operate. A low pressure inflation system is also desirable, as use of the BCD is simplified.

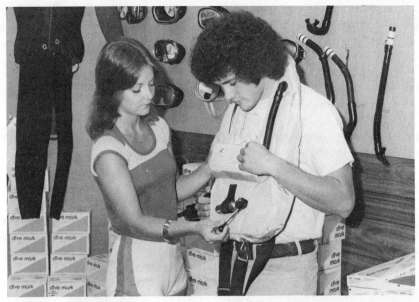

Features of a Buoyancy Control Device

Maintenance

Thoroughly rinse the inside and outside of the BCD with fresh water after use. To rinse the inside, fill it about one third full of water through the inflator hose, swish the water around the inside, then drain completely through the hose. Special maintenance may be required for some mechanisms. Follow instructional booklet recommendations. Store the BCD partially inflated.

EXPOSURE SUITS

Exposure suits for diving prevent excessive loss of body heat and provide protection from minor injuries, such as scrapes and stings. This is done by placing a protective covering over the body, to insulate and to reduce or prevent the circulation of water over the skin. Exposure suits are of value in nearly all waters, as significant body heat loss can occur in water as warm as 85° F, and protection against minor cuts and scrapes is obviously beneficial.

Draining the BCD

The most common type of exposure suit for sport diving is the wet suit, made of closed cell neoprene material and designed to fit snugly to minimize the amount of water entering the suit. The suit gets its name since some water does get inside. This water is quickly warmed by the diver, and should not circulate, or it will be replaced by cold water. A good fit will reduce circulation of water inside the suit, and, therefore, keep the diver warmer than a loosely fitting wet suit. For this reason, a snug, comfortable fit is the most important consideration in selecting a wet suit. The suit material insulates the diver from the water, and is available in various thicknesses depending on the amount of insulation needed for protection from the cold. Various suit designs are available for increased warmth if needed.

Since wet suit material is comprised of thousands of tiny closed cells, or bubbles, it is quite buoyant and will float a person very comfortably. In fact, it is very difficult to get below the surface at all without weight to offset the buoyancy of the suit.

Another type of exposure suit is the dry suit, designed to keep water from entering the suit. The dry suit uses a layer of air inside plus the suit material to insulate against cold. Dry suits are more expensive than wet suits, and are used for diving in colder waters.

Both types of suits are affected by pressure, and are compressed during descent. Air can be added to that inside a dry suit to equalize the increasing pressure during descent, but the closed cell structure of wet suit material does not lend itself to regular equalization techniques. As the volume of the wet suit is decreased due to compression, a loss of buoyancy and insulation results. The loss of buoyancy must be compensated for to regain neutral buoyancy. This is achieved through the use of the Buoyancy Control Device, which allows the diver to maintain neutral buoyancy at depth. When wearing a wet suit and descending, air needs to be added to the BCD frequently to offset the effects of pressure upon suit buoyancy.

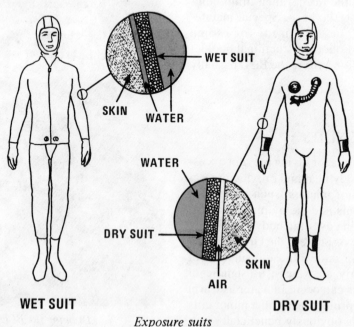

WET SUIT

SKIN   WATER

WATER

DRY SUIT

SKIN

AIR

WET SUIT   **DRY SUIT**

Exposure suits

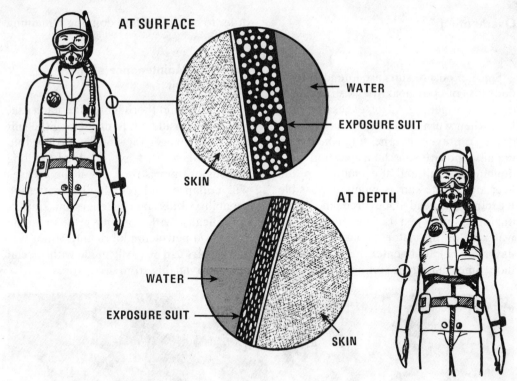

AT SURFACE

WATER

EXPOSURE SUIT

SKIN

AT DEPTH

WATER

EXPOSURE SUIT

SKIN

Suit compresses during descent due to increase in pressure.

Exposure suits are available in many styles with numerous features. Select the type and features commonly used in the area where you will be diving. The most important considerations are warmth, fit, and comfort. An exposure suit is one of the first items of equipment to obtain and can make the difference between a cold, miserable experience underwater, or enjoyment and comfort.

Hood, Boots, and Gloves

These are additional parts of an exposure suit which provide warmth and protection of the body extremities. A hood and boots are recommended for water temperatures of 70° F or colder. Both should fit snugly, but not tightly. Boots are also of value to prevent chaffing and irritation from sand or gravel captured in the fins and for walking over rough terrain to the water. Hands softened in water can be cut easily. For this reason, gloves should be worn for protection when diving, regardless of water temperature. Various designs and thicknesses are available for these items, depending on the degree of insulation needed. Gloves should be worn while learning to dive, so you will be able to handle the equipment when wearing them after training.

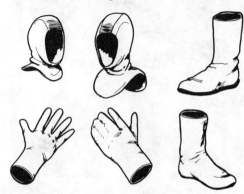

Protection for the body extremities

Overheating

Since exposure suits are intended to reduce loss of body heat, they can prevent a diver from getting rid of excessive body heat when worn out of the water on warm days. To prevent overheating when wearing an exposure suit, limit exertion while donning the suit and after suiting up, and keep out of the sun as much as possible. Keeping the head uncovered and jacket unzipped until just before entering the water helps in heat elimination. On hot days, it is helpful to enter the water one or more times during the suiting up process in order to cool off before donning remaining equipment.

Care and Maintenance of the Exposure Suit

Rinse the suit thoroughly after each use, and turn it inside out to dry. Hang the suit on a wide hanger for storing. Do not fold the suit tightly or leave it folded for long periods of time as the cells at the creases will collapse and reduce the insulating capability. Lubricate fasteners and zippers periodically with silicon spray or some other non-petroleum lubricant. Minor wet suit repairs can be easily made with special cement available from dive stores.

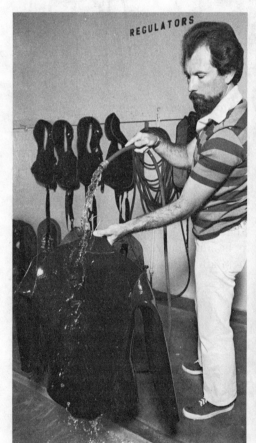
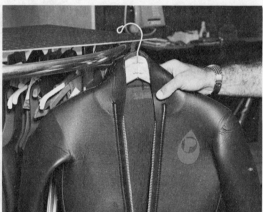
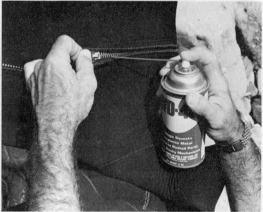

Proper exposure suit maintenance includes rinsing after use, storage without creases, and lubrication of zippers and fasteners

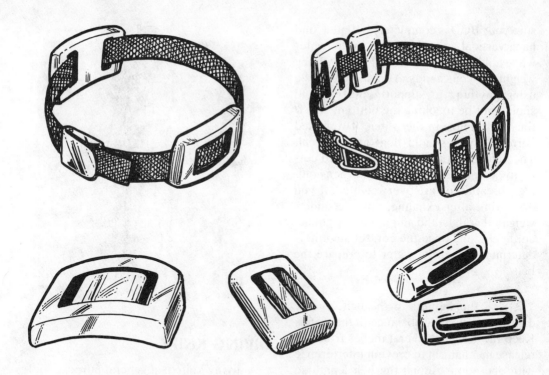

Commonly used weights, weight belts, and quick release buckles

WEIGHT BELT

Lead is quite heavy in water, and is worn on a belt by the diver to offset positive buoyancy and achieve neutral weighting. Some people are naturally buoyant and require several pounds of weight so they will not have to work constantly to stay underwater, and wearing an exposure suit will require weight in order to offset the buoyancy of the suit.

Both the lead weights and the belt are available in many shapes and styles. The most important feature is a quick release device, which can be operated simply and easily with only one hand. Since the weights are used to overcome positive buoyancy, releasing them at any time will instantly provide buoyancy. This is of value in an emergency, so you must be able

to quickly release the weight belt should the need arise. The choice of configuration for the weight belt is a matter of personal preference. Again, the type most commonly used in the local area should be a guide to aid in selection.

Preparing the weight belt for use

First you need to determine the amount of weight needed. This will depend on your physical size and weight, the equipment being used, and the density of the water. Without an exposure suit, only a few pounds of weight may be needed, if any is needed at all. With an exposure suit, approximately 10% of your body weight will be needed. To determine the amount of weight needed, wear all equipment to be used, enter water too deep to stand, be sure your BCD is completely deflated, and hang vertical and motionless in the water while holding a normal breath and with the weights in your hands. You should not be using anything to support yourself, and should not be touching the bottom. Allow time to stabilize in the water. If weighted correctly, you should float at eye level. The final test is to exhale. If weighed correctly, you will sink. If you sink when holding a breath, you are overweighted; if you don't sink after exhaling, you are underweighted. Adjust the amount of weight accordingly, and once the correct amount is determined, exit the water to prepare the belt.

Attach the weights to the belt, evenly distributing them for balance in the water. Keep the weights several inches from the release mechanism to prevent interference with operation. Adjust the belt length so only 6-8 inches of strap remain beyond the release when the belt is secured in place.

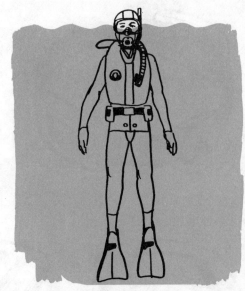

Testing buoyancy

DIVING KNIFE

A diving knife is a general purpose tool used for cutting, prying, digging, pounding, measuring, etc. It is not intended to be,

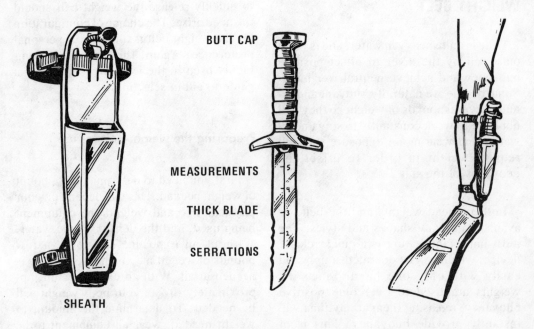

BUTT CAP

MEASUREMENTS

THICK BLADE

SERRATIONS

SHEATH

Typical diving knife. Attach the knife to the inside of the leg.

The gear bag is an essential item of equipment for divers

or should not be used as, a weapon, but should be part of standard diving equipment.

One edge of the knife should be serrated for cutting lines or rope underwater. The knife should not be extremely sharp, and is best sharpened with a file. Many divers keep another, smaller knife available for above-water use, such as cleaning game.

A sheath to hold the knife is usually provided with straps to secure it to the leg. The sheath should be positioned on the inside of the lower leg to reduce the chance of entanglement with surrounding weeds or other objects.

GEAR BAG

A gear bag is essential for transporting and temporarily storing equipment for diving. It allows a diver to keep all gear together when working in crowded areas, such as aboard a boat, and reduces confusion due to a mix-up of equipment. The bag should be sturdy and large enough to accommodate all equipment except the scuba tank and weight belt. These items would make handling of the bag difficult, and could damage other items inside. The tank and weight belt should be carried separately.

A gear bag should be packed in the reverse order in which the equipment will be needed when diving. The first item needed, such as the wet suit, should be on top, and the last items needed, such as the fins, should be at the bottom. When removing equipment after a dive, place it in the gear bag as it is removed. By learning to use a gear bag efficiently, working with equipment will be easier, and confusion will be minimized.

Equipment should be well marked for easy identification

EQUIPMENT IDENTIFICATION

All personal equipment should be marked to allow quick identification. This will reduce frustration and confusion when similar gear, adjusted to different sizes, is in use by several divers simultaneously.

Gear identification also aids in distinguishing a diver underwater. The equipment should be marked with marking paint, special crayons, colored tape, or some other means soon after being obtained. This should be part of the preparation for use for all items of personal gear.

Respiration

A problem encountered when entering water is supplying oxygen to our bodies. We are air breathing mammals, unable to obtain oxygen from water as fish can. We need to learn how we breathe, then learn the proper breathing methods for diving activities. This is part of our adaptation to the underwater environment.

GOALS

By the end of this module, you should be able to explain the benefits and hazards of hyperventilation, how to breathe efficiently while diving, how to prevent and cope with overexertion, and how to prevent choking on inhaled water.

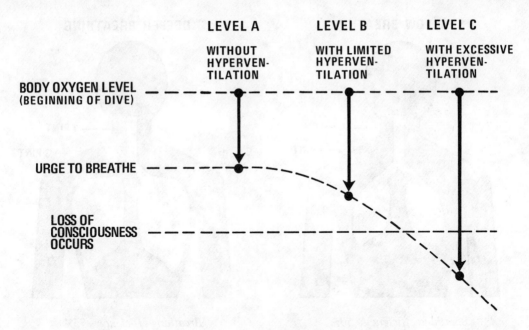

LEVEL A
WITHOUT HYPERVEN-TILATION

LEVEL B
WITH LIMITED HYPERVEN-TILATION

LEVEL C
WITH EXCESSIVE HYPERVEN-TILATION

BODY OXYGEN LEVEL
(BEGINNING OF DIVE)

URGE TO BREATHE

LOSS OF CONSCIOUSNESS OCCURS

Effects of hyperventilation (overbreathing)

HYPERVENTILATION

Breathing rapidly and deeply — known as hyperventilation — followed by breath-holding, increases the length of time you can hold a breath by prolonging the time required until you are stimulated to breathe. This technique is of value to extend breathholding *if* hyperventilation is limited to three or four breaths. However, excessive hyperventilation of more than three or four breaths can be dangerous. It is possible to breathhold until all the oxygen within you has been consumed and still have no desire to breathe because the stimulus has been prolonged too long. This results in unconsciousness, due to insufficient oxygen, occurring *without warning,* and can lead to drowning when in the water. Limited hyperventilation can be used safely to extend breathhold time, but breathing deeply and rapidly for more than three or four breaths prior to breathholding can lead to blackout underwater. Do *not* hyperventilate excessively.

Blackout can also be caused by making repeated breathhold dives without sufficient rest intervals between them. Allow at least one minute intervals between dives to prevent underwater blackout.

Another form of hyperventilation can be caused by anxiety and stress. In this situation, a person breathes rapidly, but shallowly, which will lead to respiratory difficulty. With proper techniques, stress and anxiety can be avoided in diving. If you should find yourself breathing rapidly and shallowly, simply control your breathing to prevent any difficulty. Force yourself to breathe slowly and deeply and to take it easy, and the anxiety will soon pass.

BREATHING EFFICIENCY

Respiration does not take place in the air spaces in our mouth, throat, and windpipe. These tubes, which route air to and from

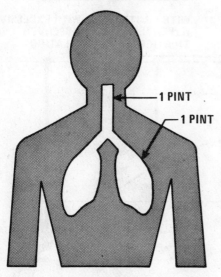

1 PINT

1 PINT

Breathing efficiency - 50%

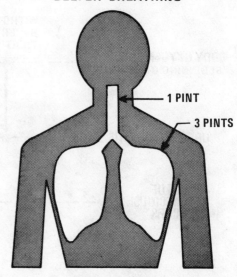

1 PINT

3 PINTS

Breathing efficiency - 75%

our lungs, and have a volume of approximately one pint, are termed dead air spaces. When breathing shallowly, or inhaling about two pints of air, only one pint of the air reaches our lungs, as the other pint remains in the dead air space. This means only 50% of the air we breathe in is being used. If we breathe more deeply, however, or about four pints, three pints of the air reach the lungs, allowing 75% of the air breathed to be used. This is more efficient breathing.

It is important for us to breathe efficiently when diving, whether breathing through a snorkel or with scuba. This equipment increases the amount of dead air space, so the amount of air which must be moved to get fresh air into our lungs and stale air out is also increased. The proper breathing pattern for diving is consistently slow and deep. Using scuba, we should breathe in slower and deeper than normal, and exhale slower and a little more than normal. When using a snorkel, we also inhale slowly and deeply, but may need to exhale rapidly and sharply from time to

time to blow water clear of the tube. Breathing efficiently and limiting your activity will maintain a feeling of comfort in breathing, while overexerting creates a feeling of air starvation.

OVEREXERTION

If a person works too hard while in or under the water, such as swimming against a current, carrying excessive weight, or pursuing game, overexertion will result. Symptoms are extreme fatigue, labored breathing or a feeling of suffocation, weakness, and a tendency to panic. Prevention is best. Know your physical limits and pace your activity to avoid breathlessness. Move slowly and avoid hard exertion while diving. Should you experience symptoms of overexertion, stop all activity, breathe deeply and rest. Hold onto some object for support if possible. If at the surface, establish buoyancy and stop all swimming movements. Recover completely, then proceed at a slower pace.

Move slowly and avoid hard exertion while diving

AIRWAY CONTROL

You will also learn how to breathe without sucking water down your throat when small amounts are present in the equipment, such as in the snorkel tube. If you breathe in slowly, water may enter the mouth, but will not be pulled into the airways. The water can then be expelled from the mouth. Also, placing the tip of your tongue on the roof of the mouth when taking initial breaths forms a splashboard for droplets of water entering. Remember to take the first breaths cautiously after clearing the snorkel or scuba mouthpiece of water, and to breathe in slowly. These methods will help prevent taking in water and choking. This skill, called airway control, is quickly learned, and is important for divers to develop. If, in spite of airway control techniques, you should still inhale some water and choke, you can cough through the mouthpiece of the snorkel or the regulator and can recover quickly if you swallow.

BREATHING GOALS

You must learn to control your breathing for diving — to limit hyperventilation within safe limits for breathholding, to breathe slowly and deeply for efficiency, to breathe all the time when using scuba, to prevent overexertion, and to develop airway control.

Now that you are aware of some effects of water on a person, the equipment needed for skin diving and the purpose of the equipment, and how to breathe properly, it is appropriate to consider information on how to use the various items of equipment needed by a skin diver.

EQUIPMENT PREPARATION

All personal gear should be prepared in
advance, as previously noted. It should be
properly adjusted, and marked for easy
identification. This will save time and reduce confusion during water sessions.
Other gear, such as the Buoyancy Control
Device and weight belt, should be adjusted
prior to suiting up, so the suiting up process
will go quickly and smoothly without delays
once begun.

ADJUSTING THE BCD

The harness should be adjusted to feel
snug and comfortable. This adjustment
should be made with the BCD fully inflated, as the adjustment may change due
to inflation. Examine the various controls
and familiarize yourself with their operation. Deflate the BCD after familiarization
and adjustment.

ADJUSTING THE WEIGHT BELT

If a weight belt is to be used, the instructor will tell you approximately how much
weight to use initially. Distribute the
weights evenly on the belt, and adjust the
belt length to be no more than 6 to 8 inches
longer than needed to fit your waist.

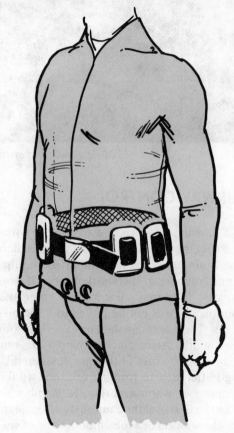

Proper adjustment of the weight belt

PUTTING ON EQUIPMENT

Always wait until your Instructor tells
you to don equipment, and then put on

only the gear specified. The following information is intended to make donning of the various items of gear easier for you. Additional advice and suggestions will be provided by your Instructor.

Wet Suit

Boots are the first items donned (except when exposure suit pants are worn, then the pants are donned before the boots). Work the boots on slowly, a little at a time, wiggling and twisting the foot into the foot pocket as you work the top of the boot up onto the ankle.

Work boots on gradually. Wetting them first may help

Wet suit jackets or vests may be used during confined water training to prevent chilling, and to allow more familiarization with their use, handling, and effect of buoyancy. If a jacket is used, put it on one arm at a time, working each arm all the way up to the arm pit. Pull or stretch seams as little as possible. It may seem difficult to get the jacket on at first, but this will become easier with experience. Next, fasten the crotch flap to hold the sides together at the bottom, then zip up the jacket. With a proper fit, it will feel quite snug and restrictive at first, but this feeling will be relieved somewhat in the water, and even more as you get used to the suit. If a jacket is not used, it is recommended a sweat shirt or tee shirt be worn to keep the tank straps from chaffing your shoulders.

When donning the wet suit jacket, work one sleeve all the way onto the arm before putting the rest of the jacket on

Buoyancy Control Device

After donning the wet suit jacket (if used), put on the BCD and recheck the adjustment.

Weight Belt

Grasp the weight belt by the end without the buckle, and get used to handling it this way, as the weights may slide off the belt when in the water if you hold the belt by the buckled end. To don the belt on land, hold the buckle end in your left hand and the other end in your right hand and step over it, then bend over and position the belt across the small of the back. This will relieve the tension on the front of the belt and make it easier to position, tighten, and secure. The same idea applies when in the water. Lay face down on the surface or on the bottom to secure the weight belt. A right-hand release of the weight belt is standard, so position the release to operate that way. Generally, if you have the buckle on the left-hand side, the release will operate to the right. Be sure the weight belt is over all other straps and harnesses so it is clear to drop. The belt should fit snugly, but not tightly. Loosen and secure the

Step over belt

Putting on the weight belt. (BCD not worn to permit better view of procedure.)

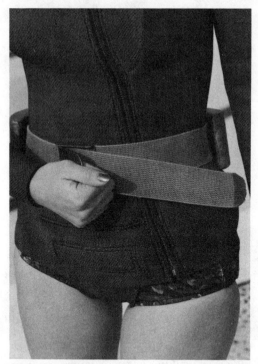
Right hand release

weight belt several times until you can do so confidently and without looking. This is necessary, as it is difficult to see your waist in the water, especially with the BCD inflated. Make sure the weights are evenly distributed, and are not interfering with the operation of the quick release mechanism. It also helps to have the weights slightly forward of the hips, as this makes the diver more stable when swimming.

Mask and Snorkel

Fog will form on the inside of the mask lens unless the lens is coated with a substance to prevent fogging. Commercial anti-fog compounds are available, and saliva works well. Put some compound or saliva on the lens, rub it in and around, then rinse the mask quickly with water. This should prevent fogging unless the oily film on a new mask lens has not been removed, or the mask has been flooded several times, removing the anti-fog coating.

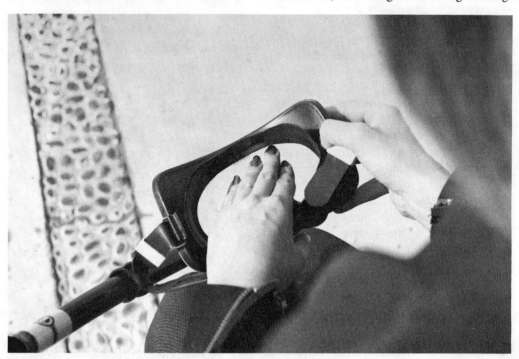
Mask defogging. Rub compound or saliva over entire lens surface

To don the mask, hold it firmly in place with one hand while positioning the strap with the other hand

To don the mask, position it in place on the face and hold it there with one hand, while using the other hand to position the strap over the crown of the head.

Mask strap adjustment and snorkel adjustment should be correct, but check them after donning the mask.

Develop the habit of keeping the mask in place, once positioned, until exiting the water. Propping the mask on the forehead is a habit which should be avoided because it can result in losing the mask when diving in open water. In many areas this is used and recognized as a distress signal.

Fins

Wet the feet or boots and the fins to make donning the fins easier. Have someone steady you as you put on one fin at a time as shown in the illustration. Be sure to work your foot well into the foot pocket

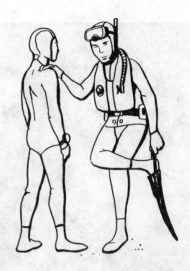

Be sure you can control your balance when donning fins

before pulling the heel portion of the fin into place.

Always put your fins on at the water's edge, as walking in fins is clumsy and can be hazardous. If you must walk with fins, either in or out of the water, shuffle them, and walk backwards or sideways looking over the shoulder.

Avoid walking with fins. If necessary to do so, walk backwards or sideways, watch over your shoulder, and shuffle your feet

Gear Inspection

Have someone inspect your equipment prior to entering the water to make sure the gear is complete and donned correctly. Diving is always done in buddy teams. Develop the habit of checking your buddy's gear for correctness, function, and to familiarize yourself with the location and operation of controls and releases, and require your buddy to do the same for you.

Always inspect each other's equipment before entering the water.

Skin Diving Skills

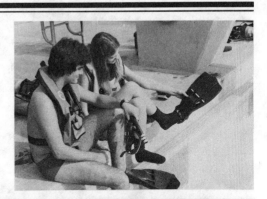

When proficient in these skills, you will be prepared to gain skin diving experience in open water under the supervision of your Instructor.

GOALS

Your goal is to be able to perform the following skills properly and easily by the end of the first Skill Development Session:

1. Swimming with fins (100 yards)
2. Surface Snorkeling (50 yards)
3. Surface Dives (Repeatedly)
4. Underwater Swimming (50 feet)
5. Ascents (Repeatedly)
6. Snorkel Clearing by Blast and Displacement methods (Repeatedly)
7. Buoyancy Control Device Inflation and Deflation (Repeatedly)

ENTERING THE WATER

Special entry techniques are needed for certain diving situations; but, in general, the best entry is the easiest entry, with as little impact with the water as possible. If you can wade in, or lower yourself in, that's fine. The idea is to get in without becoming disoriented or displacing any equipment.

Some general rules for entries include:
1. Be sure the entry point is clear.
2. Have the Buoyancy Control Device about 50% inflated to provide immediate buoyancy.
3. Be sure your buddy is prepared to enter.
4. Hold your face mask firmly in place if there is a possibility of it becoming dislodged.
5. After entering, clear the entry area, wait for your buddy, and watch while your buddy enters.

Special entry techniques will be covered later with scuba skills.

USE OF THE SNORKEL

The snorkel is going to allow you to lie face down, completely motionless, and breathe. This basic resting position is very stable and comfortable, and is much easier than treading water. You want to develop the habit of assuming the resting position at the surface when skin diving, as it conserves energy. If you must come upright in the water to talk or look around, inflate your BCD to provide support and conserve energy.

Remember to breathe slowly, deeply, and cautiously through the snorkel. Bite gently on the mouthpiece grippers, letting the lips seal the mouthpiece and hold it in place. Whenever you put a mouthpiece into your mouth, be sure to exhale before trying to inhale, in case some water might be present.

When you go beneath the surface, water will enter the snorkel. To clear this water upon surfacing, simply exhale forcefully and sharply into the snorkel. This will

Controlled Sitting Entry. Simply turn and gently lower yourself into the water.

The standard snorkeling position

"blast" the water up and out of the tube, clearing it of water. This blast method of clearing will remove nearly all the water from the snorkel. The small amount remaining will be of little concern if you will inhale slowly and cautiously. When "blast" clearing a snorkel, the exhalation must be quick and forceful, much like shooting a pea shooter. This method will also work if any water sloshes into the snorkel when swimming at the surface. Snorkel clearing will become automatic with experience.

"Blast" clearing the snorkel

If you are unable to clear the snorkel sufficiently with the first exhalation, it is possible, and really quite simple, to take another breath and clear the snorkel, in spite of the fact that water is in the tube when you are trying to inhale. Simply inhale very slowly, essentially "bubbling" the air through the water until you have enough air in your lungs to blow the water

out of the snorkel. The ability to do this demonstrates airway control and proper snorkel clearing techniques.

There is another method of snorkel clearing, called the displacement method, which is more effective once developed. This involves inverting the snorkel underwater by looking up and exhaling a small amount of air into it, which displaces the water inside. By keeping your head tilted back and the snorkel inverted as you ascend, the snorkel will remain clear of water due to the air inside. At the surface, the head is rolled forward while exhaling to keep water out of the snorkel. When done properly, no water will remain inside the snorkel, and less effort is required than when using the blast clearing method.

Displacement clearing the snorkel, which is easier and more effective than "Blast" clearing

USE OF FINS

The standard kick for diving is the flutter kick, but it is different than the short, quick flutter kick used when swimming. When using fins, slow the kick and lengthen the stroke. The idea is to have the fins pointed behind you and to move them slowly and powerfully up and down from the hip. The legs are extended and the knees bend only slightly. The power stroke is downward, and if kicking properly, you will feel the pull of the tendons on the top of your foot where it is joined to the ankle.

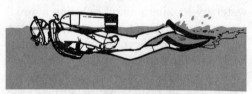

The fins only provide propulsion when pushing against water, so keep them below water when swimming at the surface. Kick down further and up less, and arch the back upward slightly to force the legs downward. It is also possible and practical to swim on your back or side at the surface while using the flutter kick. Both of these methods allow a wider kick stroke while the fins remain underwater.

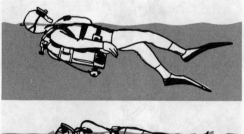

Variations of the flutter kick for surface swimming.

The flutter kick. Note the wide stroke, extended legs, and hands at the sides.

Speed is not the objective in swimming with fins, so don't swim rapidly. Also, arm movements actually reduce momentum underwater when fins are used, so keep your arms still, either extended in front or trailing at your sides.

BUOYANCY CHECK

As previously mentioned, adjust weights as you float at eye level while holding a normal breath. A complete exhalation should cause you to sink. This is neutral weighting, which allows you to maintain a position in the water without constant exertion. Be sure your BCD is completely deflated when making the buoyancy check.

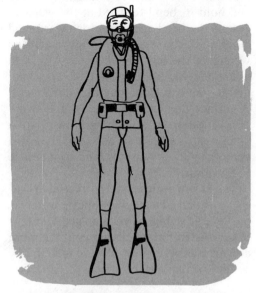

Proper weighting for neutral buoyancy.

USE OF THE BUOYANCY CONTROL DEVICE

You will want to learn quickly to inflate the BCD orally while at the surface and to deflate it before going underwater; it will allow you to remain upright at the surface to rest, talk, listen, or make equipment adjustments without having to tread water. When at the surface, you should be in the snorkel resting position, or should have your BCD inflated for surface resting.

To orally inflate the BCD, take a breath, place the mouthpiece in your mouth, open the inflation valve (usually done by depressing a button), and exhale into the device. Only exhale about 2/3 of the air in your lungs into the BCD. Your mouth and the inflator do not need to be above the surface during inflation. In fact, it requires energy to lift yourself out of the water for this, and that energy should be conserved. Simply lift your chin to take a breath, then put your face back into the water and exhale into the mouthpiece below the surface. Do this several times and you will be sufficiently buoyant to keep your head above water without kicking.

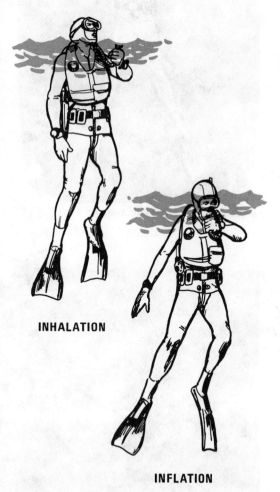

INHALATION

INFLATION

Inflation of the BCD at the surface

To deflate the BCD, simply operate the exhaust valve while making it the highest point. This is as simple as it sounds, yet people sometimes try to exhaust the BCD in positions were the air cannot escape.

Deflation of the BCD on descent

Surface swimming for distance is easier if the BCD is only partially inflated. If fully inflated, it is difficult to assume a facedown position. Inflating the BCD about half full is generally adequate for surface swimming or resting.

SURFACE DIVES

To get below the surface as a skin diver, have the BCD deflated, hyperventilate not more than 3 or 4 times, take a large breath and hold it, bend forward at the waist to extend the head and arms downward, and quickly lift the legs out of the water. The weight of the legs above water will push you underwater and when the fins submerge you can kick your way downward. A surface dive can be done from a swimming position or a stationary position. A swimming surface dive is easier, but a stationary dive is useful, and should also be developed.

The key to a successful surface dive is to get as much of your legs above water as possible. The higher you can get your legs out of the water and above you, the more downward force you will have to help you get below the surface.

Have the BCD partially inflated for surface swimming.

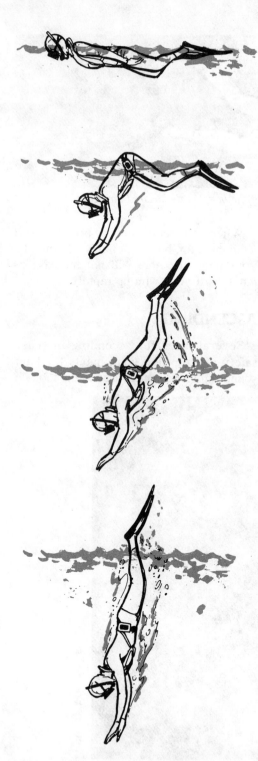

DESCENDING

As you descend, you will feel the effects of pressure on your mask and in your ears even in shallow water. Equalize these pressures by exhaling slightly into your mask and then blocking the nostrils while attempting to exhale through the nose to add air to the air spaces inside the ears.

Equalization during descent

Equalization, especially of ears, should be done every 2 or 3 feet and should not be delayed until discomfort is felt. In fact, if you wait until pain is felt before attempting to equalize, you will probably not be able to do so. It is necessary to stay ahead of pressure increases, so equalize early and often during descent. Practice and experience will make equalizing become an automatic reaction.

UNDERWATER SWIMMING

When underwater, relax as much as possible and swim slowly to conserve oxygen. Most people can stay below the surface for 30 seconds easily, and in 30 seconds quite a bit can be accomplished. Keep all the air in your lungs until clearing the snorkel on ascent.

Head first surface dive for skin diving.

SECTION 1   41

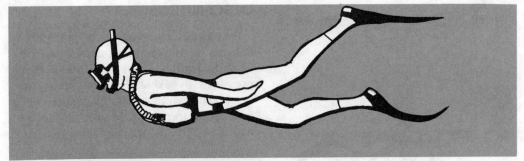

Control direction underwater by angling the body in the desired direction.

Direction is controlled by directing the trunk of the body. If you arch your back upwards, you will go up; if you arch it downward, you will go down; if angled to the right, you will turn to the right; and so on. Arm movements are helpful for making sharp turns. On your descent, go straight down, then turn 90 degrees and level off. This is more efficient than angling to the bottom.

When you feel the urge to breathe, start swimming up, but don't hurry. If you take your time, the urge will not increase as much as if you swim up rapidly.

ASCENDING

Several rules for ascending increase safety and develop good habits for later scuba skills. Whenever ascending, look up

Photo by Eric Frehsee

When ascending, look up, reach up, then come up.

and around, and extend one hand overhead for protection from overhead objects. It is also advisable to make at least one rotation during the ascent to see what is around and behind you. When ascending, remember to look up, reach up, and then come up. Clear your snorkel by the desired displacement method when ascending. After surfacing, make another rotation to check position and surroundings.

WATER IN THE MASK

When diving, some water may leak into the mask for various reasons, such as laughing. While at the surface, simply pull the bottom skirt of the mask away from your face and allow the water to run out. You can also tilt the mask to achieve the same result. Do not remove the mask; this is unnecessary and wastes time and energy. Later you will learn to clear the water from the mask underwater by displacing the water with air, but for skin diving, the draining method at the surface is sufficient.

A skin diver simply drains any water which may leak into the mask.

EXITS

There are some exit procedures for diving that you should begin to develop early. Generally, divers exit from deep water one at a time and keep all gear in place until ready to exit. If climbing a ladder, remove fins and hand them up, or carry them with

you. Keep clear of the exit until the person getting out before you has cleared the exit area. Clear all personal gear from the exit area immediately upon emerging from the water.

A ladder is frequently used for exits by divers.

GENERAL CARE AND MAINTENANCE OF DIVING EQUIPMENT

Rinse equipment with fresh water as soon as possible after use in salt water, dirty water, or pool water. The ideal method is to soak the equipment in fresh water to dissolve salt and dirt. After soaking, the gear should be rinsed well.

Avoid exposing equipment to sunlight for prolonged periods.

Store diving equipment in a cool area away from smog, gas, or oil fumes. If the gear needs to be stored for more than a few months, make sure it is completely dry, then seal it inside plastic bags.

Read and follow the manufacturer's instructions and recommendations regarding care of the equipment.

Rinse equipment with fresh water after use.

SECTION 2

- ## Mechanics of Pressure
- ## Scuba Equipment
- ## Communications
- ## The Buddy System
- ## Using Scuba Equipment
- ## Scuba Diving Skills

Mechanics of Pressure

In the first section, we learned some effects of pressure. In this section we will learn: (1) the relationships between pressure, volume and density; (2) their effects on a diver; and (3) how to deal with these effects.

GOALS

By the end of this module, you should be able to explain pressure, volume, and density relationships due to pressure; their effects on a diver; and how to prevent discomfort or injury due to pressure changes.

PRESSURE/VOLUME/DENSITY RELATIONSHIPS

The weight of the atmospheric pressure around us is relatively constant and is a standard reference for pressure measurement, referred to as one atmosphere of pressure. In sea water, pressure increases by one atmosphere for each 33 feet so at a depth of 33 feet, the total pressure exerted on a diver is two atmospheres, compared to one atmosphere at the surface. Pressure increases at a rate of one atmosphere (ATM) for each additional 33 feet as shown.

DEPTH	PRESSURE
0′	1 ATM
33′	2 ATM
66′	3 ATM
99′	4 ATM

Figure A

Notice that the total pressure is twice as great at 33 feet than at the surface, three times as great at 66 feet, and so forth. This pressure pushes inward on flexible air spaces, compressing them, and reducing their volume. The reduction of air volume is in proportion to the increase in pressure, as shown when a heavy inverted bell full of air is lowered in water.

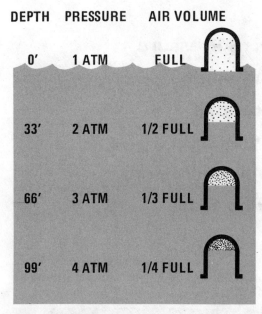

Figure B. Effects of increasing pressure on volume.

When the total pressure doubles, the air volume is halved; when the pressure triples, the volume is reduced to one third; etc.

The density of the air in the air space is also affected by pressure. As the volume of the air space is reduced due to compression, the density of the air increases as the air is squeezed into a smaller space. No air is lost, it is simply compressed. The air density is also proportional to pressure. When the total pressure is doubled, air density is also doubled; when tripled, air density is tripled; etc.

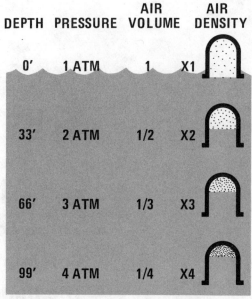

Figure C. Effects of increasing pressure on air density.

To maintain the air space at its original volume when the pressure is increased, air must be added. This is the concept of equalization of pressure. The amount of air required to be added is proportional to the pressure as shown.

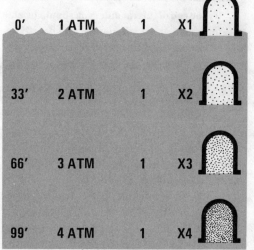

Figure D.

Air within an air space will expand as the pressure is reduced. If no air has been added to the air space, the air will simply expand to its original volume upon reaching the surface. In Figure B, the air compressed in the bell during descent will expand on ascent in proportion to the pressure.

If air has been added to an air space to equalize pressure at depth, this air will also expand as pressure is reduced during ascent. The amount of expansion is again proportional to the pressure. In an open container, such as the bell, the expanding air will simply bubble out the opening, so the original volume is maintained constantly during the ascent. In a closed, flexible container, however, the volume will increase as the pressure is reduced. If the volume exceeds the capacity of the container, the container may be ruptured due to the expansion of air. This effect can be noted on a plastic bag filled with air at 99 feet and released.

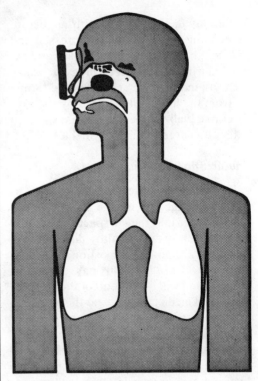

Diver's air spaces

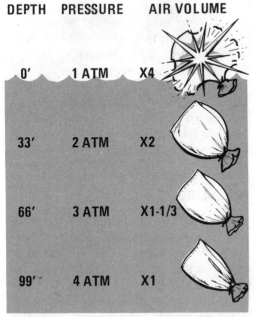

DEPTH	PRESSURE	AIR VOLUME
0'	1 ATM	X4
33'	2 ATM	X2
66'	3 ATM	X1-1/3
99'	4 ATM	X1

Figure E. Effects of decreasing pressure on volume.

EFFECTS OF INCREASING PRESSURE

Now let's see how these relationships between pressure, volume, and density affect a diver. During descent, pressure increases and pushes inward on body air spaces. If an air space is not equalized, a condition known as a squeeze will result. A diver can feel a squeeze in ears, sinuses, and mask. When a squeeze affects an air space in direct contact with the body, pain will result unless air is added to the air space to make the air pressure inside equal to the total pressure outside. This is equalization, and you have already experienced it to a limited extent during the first Skill Development Session.

The effect of a squeeze does not apply to the lungs, however, which are flexible and can be compressed with no consequence as long as they are filled with air before descending. They will be compressed and reduced in volume during descent, and expand during ascent, returning to nearly their original volume at the surface. Some air from the lungs will be used by the skin diver to equalize other air spaces, since no external source of air is available.

Equalization Techniques

Blocking the nose and attempting to exhale through it with the mouth closed will force air into the air spaces inside the ears and sinuses in a healthy diver. A person with a cold or congestion will have swollen or plugged air passages and equalization will be difficult or impossible. The use of medication to clear the openings in order to dive is not advisable, and can lead to difficulty if the medication wears off while under pressure. Swallowing and wiggling the jaw from side to side are effective at times as equalization techniques, but nose blocking is still the most effective method.

Equalize pressure every few feet while descending, before discomfort is felt. If pain is present, continued efforts to equalize will be ineffective, as the pressure

Equalize pressure early and often during descent

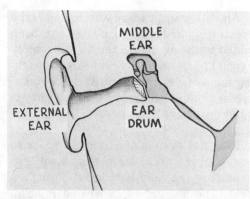

Air spaces inside the ears

will actually hold the passageways shut. Physical damage will occur with any further descent. Ascending a few feet will relieve the discomfort by reducing the pressure and allowing equalization. The descent may then be continued. If equalization cannot be achieved, the dive must be discontinued. Equalization of ears and sinuses becomes easier with experience.

The external ear canal can also be affected by pressure if sealed. Do not wear ear plugs when diving, and be careful that a hood with a smooth inside surface does not seal the ears during descent. If this is a problem, simply pull the hood away momentarily to allow the air to escape, thereby eliminating the air space.

The mask squeeze can be felt by a pulling sensation on the face and eyes, and can be relieved simply by exhaling into the mask. Mask equalization will become automatic with experience.

EFFECTS OF DECREASING PRESSURE

For the skin diver, there are no effects of decreasing pressure due to ascent. Air expanding inside the ears, sinuses, and mask escapes easily, and the lungs merely expand back to the original volume. If, due to expanding air, you should feel any discomfort in air spaces during ascent, ascend as slowly as possible, then discuss the problem with your Instructor after surfacing.

A different situation exists for the scuba diver, however. Scuba equipment not only allows us to breathe while underwater, but also delivers air automatically at the pressure equal to that upon us at any depth. This means our lungs will be at their normal volume while at depth and will expand upon ascent. If the diver breathes normally, keeping the airway to the lungs open, this expanding air will escape. But, if the diver closes off the airway by holding the breath, the lungs will expand just like the plastic bag in Figure E, and lung rupture can occur without warning. The most important rule in scuba diving is to breathe continuously and never hold your breath. There is a natural tendency to hold the breath underwater, and this tendency must be changed for diving; lung expansion injuries are possible in very shallow water and are extremely hazardous. To prevent these injuries, simply don't hold your breath during ascent. Breathe all the time!

Other air spaces generally pose no problems during ascent. However, it is possible for expanding air to be trapped in ears, sinuses, or under an inadequate tooth filling. Gas formed in the stomach or intestines during diving can also expand during ascent. These situations, although uncommon, cause discomfort if they occur. Should you feel discomfort due to pressure during ascent, slow or stop the ascent and allow the trapped gas to work its way out. If severe or repeated instances occur, see a diving physician to determine the cause.

EFFECT OF INCREASED AIR DENSITY

From Figure D, it is easy to determine that more air is required to fill an air space as the pressure increases. With this concept applied to breathing, one can also understand how a given quantity of air in a scuba tank will be used more quickly at

depth. For example, three times as much air is needed to fill the lungs with air at a depth of 66 feet as would be required at the surface. Therefore, an air supply would last only one third as long at 66 feet as at the surface.

Another effect of increased air density at depth is its effect on ease of breathing. Dense air is harder to get in and out of the lungs than air at normal surface pressure. Deep, slow breathing is the most efficient method of respiration for breathing dense air, and is another reason for breathing in this fashion while underwater.

SUMMARY

Changes in pressure, either increasing or decreasing, affect the diver in several ways. Through proper techniques of equalization and breathing, internal and external pressures can be kept in equilibrium, so discomfort or injury due to mechanical pressure changes need not occur.

When using scuba, remember to exhale or breathe continuously to prevent lung injury during ascent.

Scuba Equipment

The skin diver's excursion beneath the surface is limited to the length of time the breath can be held. Scuba equipment allows the diver to extend time underwater by providing a portable air supply. Scuba equipment consists of a tank to store compressed air, a valve to regulate the flow of air to the regulator, a back pack to hold the tank on the diver's back, a regulator to control the flow of air to the diver, and a submersible pressure gauge to allow monitoring of the air supply. Scuba is simple, yet remarkable, in that it delivers air on demand and equal to the pressure exerted upon a diver. Sport divers use only open circuit scuba where the air is breathed from a tank and exhausted into the water. Closed circuit scuba, such as rebreathers, require very special maintenance and training and should *not* be used for recreational diving.

GOALS

By the end of this module, you should be able to demonstrate a familiarity with standard scuba configurations, and should be able to explain the general care and maintenance for scuba equipment.

SCUBA TANKS

A scuba tank is a cylindrical metal container used to store safely high pressure air for breathing. Scuba cylinders are available in a variety of sizes and various pressure ratings. Their capacities are stated in terms of the number of cubic feet of compressed air they can contain. Common sizes are 38, 50, 71.2, and 80 cubic feet. Tanks may be obtained in double units for special applications, but single tanks are the most popular. The standard 71.2 cubic foot steel tank or 80 cubic foot aluminum tank contain air approximately equal in volume to that occupied by a telephone booth. The air is compressed into a space about two feet long and about one half foot in diameter. As air is compressed into a smaller space, its pressure increases. The pressure in scuba tanks may be higher than 4,000 pounds per square inch, but typical pressure ratings are 1,800, 2,250, and 3,000.

Both steel and aluminum tanks are available. Compressed gas containers are subject to regulations established by the Department of Transportation (DOT), and must pass periodic pressure tests. Either steel or aluminum tanks are acceptable as long as they meet current DOT requirements.

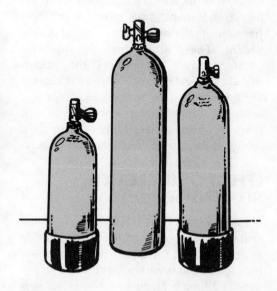

Common sizes of scuba tanks

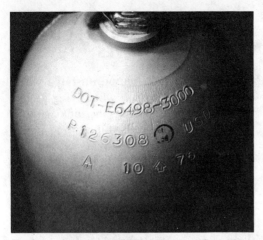

Tank markings provide important information

Tank equipped with a boot. Also note the decal which indicates the tank has had an internal inspection.

The Department of Transportation requires certain information to be stamped onto the neck of high pressure cylinders. These markings provide information on the type of material from which the tank was made, the working pressure of the tank, and its date of manufacture. Additional markings include a serial number for identification of the tank, dates of all hydrostatic (pressure) tests, and may include manufacturer and distributor symbols. Tanks are required to be hydrostatically tested at least every five years.

Tank boots are available, which fit over the bottom end of the scuba tank to lessen the chances of damage from the tank banging into objects and to form a flat bottom for handling stability.

TANK VALVES

A tank valve is similar to a water faucet, allowing flow or shutting it off. There are two basic types of scuba valves: a K-valve, which is a simple on-off valve, and a J-valve, with a built-in reserve mechanism intended to signal when tank pressure is low. The J-valve contains a spring-operated shutoff valve, which is held open

Standard tank K-valve

J-valve; recognized by the reserve lever

by tank pressure until the pressure reaches 300 to 500 psi. At that point, the spring is strong enough to start closing the valve and breathing resistance increases to signal the diver of low tank pressure. The diver then pulls a reserve lever down, which manually compresses the shutoff valve spring and restores normal air flow. A reserve lever should be in the up position at the start of the dive and pulled down when breathing becomes difficult. A diver should not rely on a reserve valve to alert one of an air supply depletion, because the lever may not be placed in the proper position at the start of a dive, or may be bumped down accidently while diving. Other options to monitor tank pressure are available and will be presented in this section.

A safety feature required on all valves is a burst disk to relieve dangerously high pressure in a tank. This prevents a tank explosion from overfilling or from expansion of air in the tank due to excessive heat.

HANDLING, CARE, AND MAINTENANCE OF SCUBA TANKS AND VALVES

Scuba tanks are heavy; unstable when upright, tending to roll when lying down. When being transported, the tanks should be blocked to prevent rolling; and if left standing upright, should be secured to keep them from falling or being knocked over. A falling or rolling tank can cause damage to the tank valve or to objects with which it comes in contact, including people. Keep tanks secure, and don't leave them standing unattended.

Tanks are filled with totally dry air. Because of the high oxygen content inside a scuba tank, moisture will cause rust or corrosion to occur rapidly. It is important to exclude water from scuba tanks. The best way to do this is never to allow the tank to be emptied completely except for inspections and servicing. If the tank should somehow be completely exhausted, even

Block scuba tanks securely when transporting them

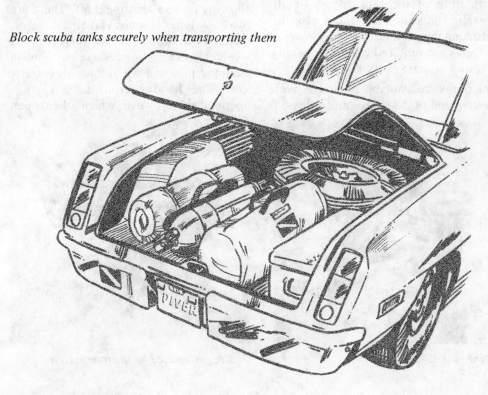

when in the water, close the valve immediately to prevent moisture from entering. It is possible for water to get into an empty tank through the regulator, so having a regulator attached is not a safeguard. Because tanks are susceptible to rust and corrosion, it is strongly recommended they be internally inspected at least once each year. The majority of professional dive stores require evidence of a current internal inspection before filling a tank. To do this, the tank must be drained of air. This should be done slowly. After the air is slowly drained from the tank, the valve is removed, and the interior is inspected using a special inspection light. This service should be performed only by professional service centers, which have the proper equipment and trained personnel.

Tanks should be stored in a cool place with a few hundred psi of air in them. Filled tanks should not be left where they can become heated, such as in the trunk of a car on a hot day, because the pressure buildup could cause the burst disk to rupture.

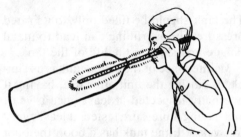

Proper tank maintenance includes annual internal inspections by trained professionals.

Tank valves should operate easily and smoothly. If there is any difficulty in operation, do not lubricate the valve, but have it serviced by a professional service center. Close valves gently, just enough to shut off the flow of air. Closing a valve tightly can damage the high pressure seat.

When a tank is to be filled, it should be filled only with compressed air for breathing, never oxygen. The tank should be cooled in water and filled slowly. The filler attachment should *not* be connected while the tank is submerged, as a small amount of water will be trapped and blown into the cylinder. If the valve is a "J" valve, the lever should be pushed down for filling.

Have scuba tanks filled properly at a reputable air station.

The tank should be filled only to its rated pressure, for overfilling can lead to metal fatigue and shorten the life of the tank.

Maintenance of the scuba tank is as simple as rinsing the unit after use, having it internally inspected at least once a year, and having it pressure tested at least every five years. If the tank has a boot, the boot should be removed periodically to make sure corrosion is not taking place under the boot. With proper care and maintenance, a scuba tank can be safely used for many thousands of dives.

BACKPACKS

A backpack is designed to hold the scuba unit securely and comfortably in place on the diver's back. This is usually done with a frame to hold the tank, two shoulder straps, and a waist strap. A number of different configurations are available, but any that satisfy the fundamental purpose are acceptable.

Desirable features include a quick release on one or both shoulder straps and on the waist strap for ease in removing the unit, and a quick-change tank retaining band so the pack can be easily changed from one tank to another.

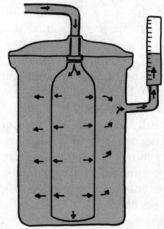

Pressure testing a scuba tank

No special maintenance is required other than rinsing and checking to see that all fittings are secure. Some types of strap releases may require occasional lubrication. The tank should not be laid on top of the backpack, and when the pack is not in use, the straps should be secured around the unit to keep them from dragging and tangling.

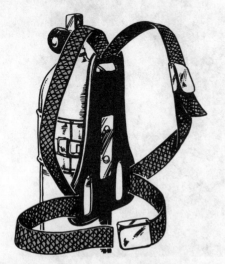

A popular type of scuba tank back pack

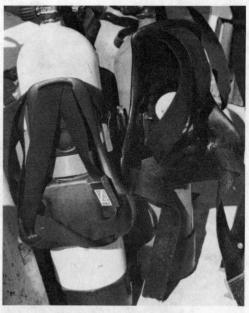

Keep pack straps secured (left) rather than allowing them to dangle (right).

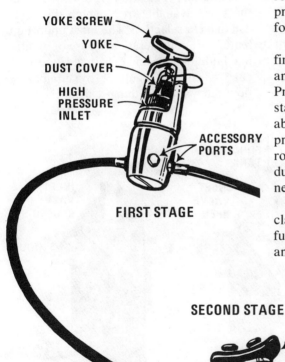

Double hose scuba regulator

REGULATORS

The scuba regulator is a very simple and reliable device with only a few moving parts; yet it can reduce the high pressure air in a scuba tank to a usable level, deliver the air only when it is needed, and deliver it at a pressure exactly equal to the surrounding or ambient pressure.

There are single hose and double hose regulators. However, the single hose regulator is used almost exclusively in sport diving. Two hose regulators require more maintenance than single hose regulators, and offer only a few advantages, which are useful only in special situations. For these reasons, only single hose regulators will be presented and are the recommended type for recreational diving.

Single hose regulators have two stages; a first stage that attaches to the scuba tank, and a second stage that has a mouthpiece. Pressure is reduced in each stage. The first stage reduces the high tank pressure of about 2,000 to 3,000 psi to an intermediate pressure of about 100 psi above the surrounding pressure. The second stage reduces the intermediate pressure to that needed for respiration.

Familiarization with regulator nomenclature will be helpful in understanding further explanations of regulator function and use:

YOKE SCREW

YOKE

DUST COVER

HIGH PRESSURE INLET

ACCESSORY PORTS

FIRST STAGE

SECOND STAGE

MOUTHPIECE

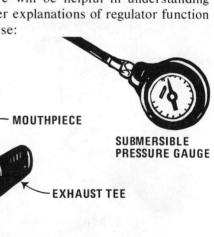

SUBMERSIBLE PRESSURE GAUGE

LOW PRESSURE HOSE

EXHAUST TEE

PURGE BUTTON

Single hose regulator nomenclature

Simplified drawings of the inside of a regulator second stage will quickly illustrate the basic functions and make use of the regulator easier. The second stage is similar to a cup covered with a sheet of rubber. Attached are a lever-operated inlet valve, a mouthpiece, and an exhaust valve. As the diver inhales, the diaphragm is sucked inward, mechanically opening the valve to deliver air to the diver. When the diver stops inhaling, air pressure inside the chamber forces the diaphragm outward and closes the valve when the internal pressure equals the ambient pressure. This is how the regulator compensates for pressure at any depth. The diver can manually control the flow of air at any time by depressing the purge button, which also opens the valve.

The exhaust valve remains closed until the diver exhales into the regulator. The exhaled air opens the exhaust valve and is released through the exhaust tee.

When the regulator is removed from the diver's mouth underwater, water will enter the second stage chamber through the mouthpiece opening, but this is of no consequence. When the diver replaces the regulator in the mouth, a small amount of air exhaled into the regulator will displace the water inside through the exhaust valve and leave the regulator clear of water for the next breath. In clearing the regulator, air will rise to the highest point, forcing water out below, so it is important to have the regulator in an upright position for clearing so all the water will be exhausted. Depressing the purge button will also clear water from the regulator second stage.

Numerous regulators with various features are available from which the diver can make a selection. The most important feature for consideration is ease of breathing, both inhaling and exhaling. Choose an easy breathing regulator by comparing flow rates and breathing resistance.

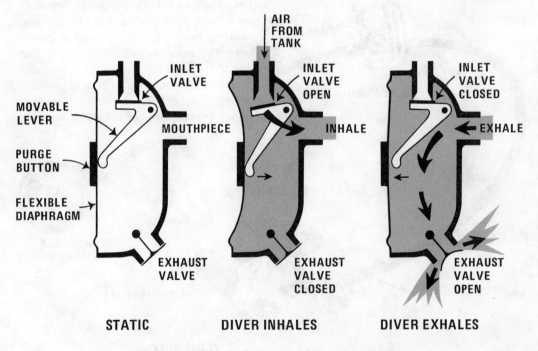

Function of the single hose regulator second stage

Regulator Care and Maintenance

Your regulator requires rinsing after every use, with warm (not hot) water whenever available, and annual servicing by a qualified professional scuba service center. Do not attempt to disassemble, repair, or lubricate scuba equipment. While it is simple, it is quite technical, and special tools, lubricants, and training are needed for proper service.

Always have the dust cover in place over the high pressure inlet any time the regulator is not attached to the scuba tank. Water — even a couple of drops — must not be allowed to enter the first stage. Be sure to dry the dust cover thoroughly before replacing it after using the regulator.

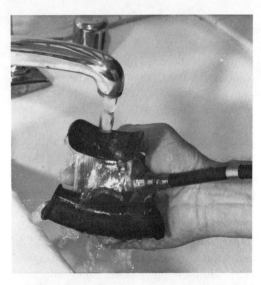

Rinsing the regulator. Use warm water and do not depress the purge button.

When rinsing the regulator it is best to soak it first, then rinse it with running water. Be sure the dust cover is securely in place. The water should be flushed through any holes in the first stage (except the high pressure inlet) and inside the second stage through the mouthpiece. Do not use high pressure water for the regulator rinsing. Be careful *not* to depress the purge button during rinsing, because this will open the second stage inlet valve and allow water to reach the first stage via the low pressure hose. It is a good precaution to attach the regulator to the scuba tank after rinsing and to purge the regulator briefly to blow out any water which may have made its way into the first stage.

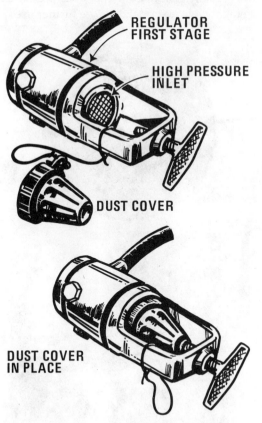

REGULATOR FIRST STAGE

HIGH PRESSURE INLET

DUST COVER

DUST COVER IN PLACE

Be sure to have the dust cover in place when the regulator is not attached to the scuba tank.

In use, keep the regulator out of sand and mud. When storing or packing the regulator, do not form tight loops in the hose. To prevent weakening of hoses, avoid pulling on them when the regulator is attached to the tank. It is better to store a regulator lying flat than to hang it by one of the stages or by the hoses. With proper care and maintenance, a scuba regulator will provide many years of dependable service.

Regulator Attachments

Ports are provided on the first stage of a regulator. There is typically one high pressure port, and one or more low pressure ports. Various items are available which attach to these ports but should be connected only by professional scuba personnel, because damage is possible if attached incorrectly.

The first of three items commonly attached to a regulator is a submersible pressure gauge, and this item should be considered a mandatory piece of equipment, not an accessory. The read out allows continuous monitoring of tank pressure while diving. Its function is the same as the gas gauge in an automobile. It enables the diver to know the pressure at the beginning of a dive, to plan the dive to end near the exit point, and to prevent running out of air. The only disadvantage of a submersible pressure gauge is that it is a passive device. Like the gas gauge in the car, it must be monitored to be a value. You need to develop the habit of looking at the submersible pressure gauge frequently while diving.

Since a submersible pressure gauge is a mandatory piece of equipment, it should be purchased at the same time as the regulator. It is a valuable and needed piece of scuba equipment. It requires no special maintenance, but is a delicate instrument and should be treated accordingly. If water is present *inside* a submersible pressure gauge, have it serviced before further use.

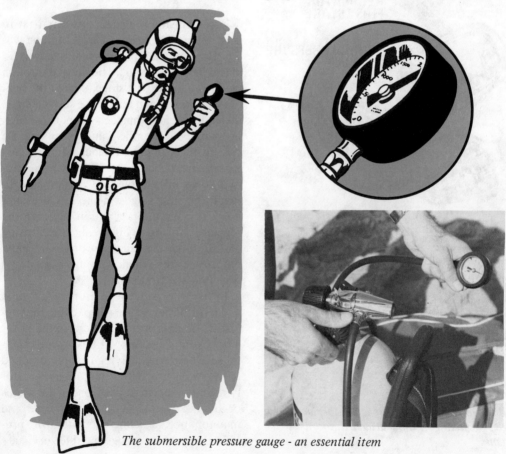

The submersible pressure gauge - an essential item

Another regulator attachment is an additional second stage, called an octopus attachment, probably named because the several hoses coming from the regulator first stage remind one of an octopus. The purpose of the additional second stage is to supply air to another diver in an emergency. While proper procedures will prevent a termination of air supply, and scuba equipment is extremely dependable, there could be an occasion where there would be a need to share air. It is easier to share air using an additional second stage than it is to pass one back and forth between divers; therefore, having a regulator equipped with an octopus attachment is recommended. The octopus attachment usually has a longer hose than the regular second stage for ease in use by another diver.

The octopus should be cared for the same as the rest of the regulator. It should be clipped to the diver for ease in location and to prevent it from dangling, but with a firm pull should come free for use.

Many Buoyancy Control Devices have a mechanism to permit inflation with low pressure air from the scuba unit. A low pressure hose connects the BCD to the regulator first stage. A low pressure BCD inflation system allows quick, efficient, one-hand buoyancy control.

In order to accommodate attachments, some regulators have multiple ports. For those with insufficient ports for all the attachments, adaptors are available which screw into a port to provide multiple outlets.

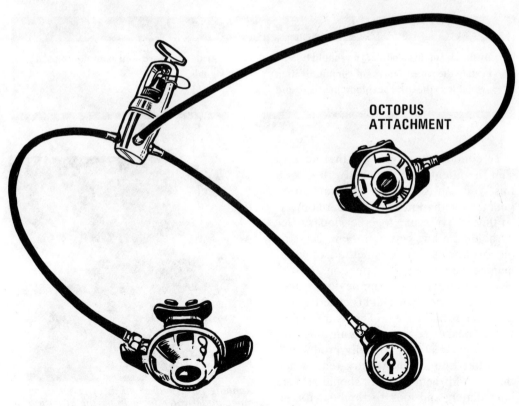

OCTOPUS
ATTACHMENT

The extra second stage or octopus attachment

Communications

Beneath the surface, voice communication is nearly impossible, except with elaborate electronic communication systems, which are prohibitively expensive for the recreational diver. More primitive methods, such as hand signals, writing on a tablet, or making noise to gain attention, are used.

GOALS

By the end of this module, you should be able to state the various forms of communication available to the diver, explain their use, and demonstrate standard and commonly used hand signals.

To communicate, you will first need to gain the attention of other divers. To do this, you can touch them, or can rap on your tank with a knife or other hard object. At times, divers stay together underwater by holding a line between them. Tugging on the line is another method of communicating and gaining attention. An underwater attention gaining device is used on some charter boats and is called an underwater recall system. This is an underwater speaker connected to an amplifier aboard the boat and typically produces a siren-like sound when activated. When this sound is heard, divers should surface immediately and look to the boat for instructions.

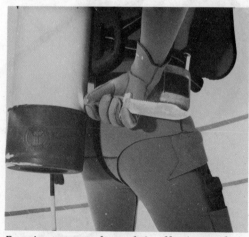

Rapping on a scuba tank is effective at short range underwater for gaining the attention of other divers.

When the attention of another diver is gained underwater, communications are possible through the use of hand signals or by writing on an underwater slate. Standard and common underwater hand signals are illustrated. Various types of underwater slates are available from retail dive stores.

Special signals are used for surface communication in diving when you are distant from the person with whom you are trying to communicate. A whistle is recommended as a standard item of equipment, because it works well to gain attention, produces a loud noise without much energy required, and its sound carries well. Several hand signals for surface communications are also illustrated. Waving an arm at the surface as a greeting should be avoided, because this is recognized as a distress signal.

Hand signals and other forms of communications should be reviewed by dive buddies before diving together as a team. Misunderstandings and confusion occur very easily with the limited communications available to divers.

An underwater slate is helpful for communications underwater.

OK signal for surface communication

OK signal with one hand occupied

NATIONAL* STANDARD HAND SIGNALS

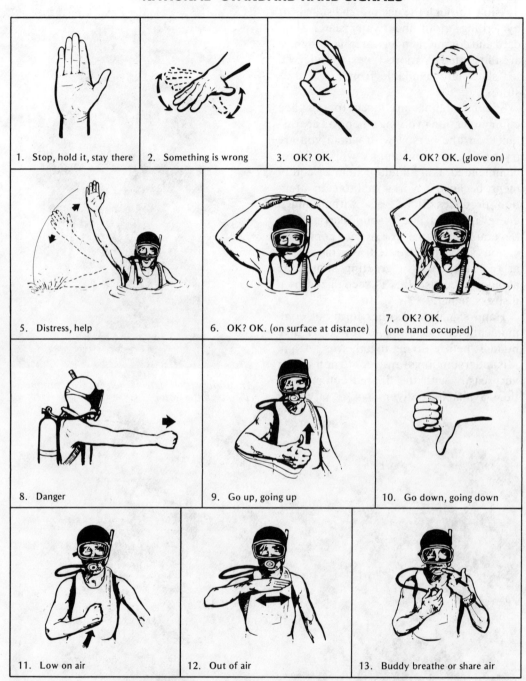

1. Stop, hold it, stay there
2. Something is wrong
3. OK? OK.
4. OK? OK. (glove on)
5. Distress, help
6. OK? OK. (on surface at distance)
7. OK? OK. (one hand occupied)
8. Danger
9. Go up, going up
10. Go down, going down
11. Low on air
12. Out of air
13. Buddy breathe or share air

＊ Hand signals 1 through 10 are recognized *internationally* in over 50 countries affiliated with CMAS—The World Underwater Federation. PADI is a member of the CMAS Technical Committee.

PADI Standard Hand Signals

COMMONLY USED HAND SIGNALS

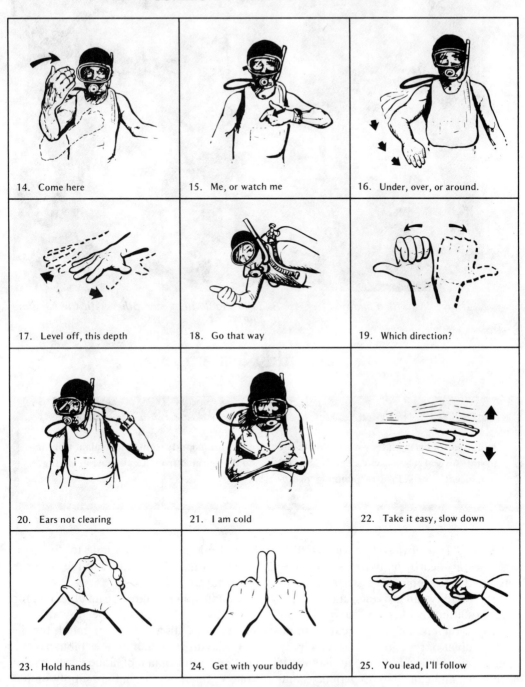

14. Come here

15. Me, or watch me

16. Under, over, or around.

17. Level off, this depth

18. Go that way

19. Which direction?

20. Ears not clearing

21. I am cold

22. Take it easy, slow down

23. Hold hands

24. Get with your buddy

25. You lead, I'll follow

PADI Standard Hand Signals

Always dive with a buddy

Buddies should help each other with the handling of equipment

The Buddy System

GOALS

By the end of his module, you should be able to state several reasons why a buddy is useful and needed, explain dive planning proce- dures for a buddy team, and explain what to do if separated from a buddy while diving.

A diver should always dive with a buddy who remains nearby at all times. Diving is safer and more enjoyable when done in teams. A buddy can provide general assistance in suiting up, checking equipment, or removing an entanglement; can remind another diver of time, depth, or air supply limits; can obtain additional assistance if necessary; and can share experiences and witness unusual occurrences. Additionally, a person feels more secure when some-

one else is present. Learning to dive as a team and maintain contact in the water is important.

Buddies should agree on an objective for each dive and work together toward that objective. With a purpose in mind, the divers should plan their dive; establish entry and exit points and techniques; a course to follow; time, depth, and air supply limits; communications; emergency procedures; and techniques of staying together, includ-

The buddy team should plan the dive, agree on the plan, and dive the plan

ing what to do if separated. Divers should plan their dive together, then dive their plan together.

During the dive, each buddy should be responsible for keeping track of the other, and should provide general assistance whenever possible. Generally speaking, divers should be separated underwater by only a few feet. Staying together is easier if the divers remain in the same position relative to one another and follow a general direction until both acknowledge a change of course. Should separation occur, buddies should search for each other not more than a minute, then surface to reunite if unable to locate one another underwater.

For safety, for practicality, and for fun, teamwork is used in diving. One of the fundamental rules of diving is "never dive alone". Choose your buddies carefully, and work together with them to develop buddy system techniques for safety and enjoyment.

Using Scuba Equipment

Your goal is to be able to perform the following skills properly and easily by the end of the second Skill Development Session:
1. Assembly of scuba equipment
2. Regulator clearing
3. Breathing without a mask
4. Mask clearing
5. Scuba descents
6. Scuba ascents
7. Regulator hose recovery
8. Feet first entries
9. Disassembly of scuba equipment

SCUBA EQUIPMENT ASSEMBLY

The back pack will usually be attached to the scuba tank and a piece of tape will be around the valve outlet. Remove the tape from the valve and discard it properly. Examine the opening in the valve. It should be surrounded by a black rubber ring, called an O-ring. This is a high pressure seal for regulator attachment. Be sure the O-ring is in place, clean, and free from cuts or nicks. You should have spare O-rings available. Your Instructor will suggest several places to carry extra O-rings. The valve opening should face toward the back pack. Stand the tank up with the pack facing away from you. Assemble the tank in this position. The pack should fit the tank securely and not move up or down. Check this before proceeding. Also, the top of the pack should generally be about even with the base of the tank valve.

Open the tank valve momentarily to blow any accumulated water or dirt out of the valve opening before attaching the regulator. The valve knob operates like a faucet, turning on counter-clockwise and off in a clockwise rotation. Unscrew the yoke screw on the regulator first stage until the dust cover can be removed, then place the regulator yoke over the tank valve matching the tank outlet to the regulator

Remove the tape from the valve

Look for and inspect the O-ring

Open the valve momentarily

inlet with the regulator hose pointing to the right. The regulator hose always goes over the right shoulder. Tighten the yoke screw onto the valve, but only finger tight. If the valve is a J-valve, the lever should be placed up at this time.

Hold the submersible pressure gauge in the left hand and facing away from you, then turn the air on slowly, listening for leaks. If a leak is present in the first stage, the O-ring may be defective. Your Instructor will show you how to inspect and replace it. A slight hissing from the second stage may stop if the purge button is pressed or the mouthpiece opening is blocked momentarily. Open the valve all the way, then back it off about a half a turn.

Check the tank pressure using the submersible pressure gauge. As a precaution, observe the gauge from an angle when out of the water. By checking the pressure rating of the tank and comparing the submersible pressure gauge reading, you can determine approximately how full the tank is. You may notice the tank pressure is somewhat less than it was when the tank was filled. The pressure in the tank is also dependent upon temperature — the tank gets warm during filling and reads a higher pressure (a few hundred psi at most) than it does after cooling. No air has been lost, the pressure has merely decreased as the temperature of the tank has decreased.

Test the regulator by depressing the purge button momentarily. The air should flow freely and stop when the button is released. Check the exhaust valve by exhaling into the regulator. Exhalation should be easy. If the exhaust valve is stuck, your Instructor will show you how to loosen it by soaking the second stage in water for a couple of minutes. If both the

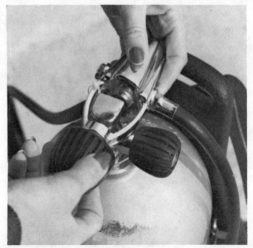

Attach the regulator to the valve. Orient the regulator hose to the right with the valve opening and back pack facing away from you

Slowly turn the air on, check the tank pressure, and . . .

Check the regulator function

Adjust the straps to estimated size

Have your buddy hold the tank while you slip into the harness

Bend forward and adjust the straps for a snug, even, comfortable fit

purge and exhaust valve function properly, take a few breaths from the regulator as a final check.

When the scuba equipment is assembled and checked, do not leave it standing unattended while you put on other equipment. Carefully lay it down, back pack up. Also, it is a good idea to lay the regulator on top of the pack to keep it off the ground and free of sand or dirt.

PUTTING ON SCUBA EQUIPMENT

Put on the wet suit first, if used, and the Buoyancy Control Device. The scuba unit is then donned, followed by the weight belt, mask and snorkel, then fins.

When putting on the scuba unit, first prepare the back pack harness. The shoulder straps should be adjusted to your approximate size, the shoulder quick release or releases should be connected, and the waist band release should be disconnected.

There are several methods of donning a scuba tank, but the recommended way is to have a buddy hold the tank while you slip

Have your buddy hand you the ends of the waist band and secure it snugly, but not tightly

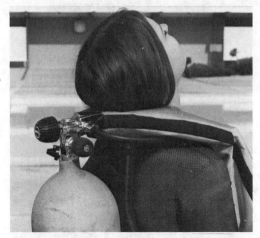

Check the height adjustment of the tank to make sure the tank won't hit you in the back of the head underwater

Don the weight belt last and over all other equipment. Hold each end of the belt and step through it

into the shoulder straps. Be sure the straps do not trap anything beneath them as the tank is lowered into place. Your buddy should then hand you each side of the waist band. At this point, bend forward and balance the tank on your back to take the strain off the harness. This allows easier adjustment and securing than when standing upright. The waist band release for the tank should open to the left, or in the opposite direction from the weight belt release.

When the tank is secure, stand upright and tilt the head back to check the height adjustment of the tank. If your head hits the valve, the tank is too high in the pack and should be repositioned.

The weight belt is put on over all other equipment. Hold the belt in both hands, step over it, then bend forward and position the belt in the small of the back under the end of the tank. Secure the weight belt with a right hand release. Be sure the regulator hoses or the submersible pressure gauge hose are not trapped under the weight belt. To prevent this, place the regulator hoses over the shoulders when putting on the weight belt.

Bend forward to allow gravity to hold the belt in place while you position and secure it. Be careful not to trap the regulator hoses under the belt

The weight belt should be secured with a right-hand release

Recovery of the regulator second stage can be accomplished by lowering the right shoulder

Recovery of the regulator can also be accomplished by reaching over the shoulder

Learn to locate the regulator hose before entering the water. You can lower the right shoulder, causing the regulator second stage to swing near your downward extended hand, or can reach over your right shoulder, grab the hose at the first stage, and follow it to the second stage. It may be necessary to lift up on the bottom of the tank with the other hand in order to reach the hose over your shoulder.

Put on your mask, snorkel, and fins at the water's edge. Before entering the water, you and your buddy should inspect all equipment on each other for correct positioning, adjustment, and function.

Scuba Diving Skills

USING SCUBA FOR THE FIRST TIME

It is a real thrill to breathe underwater for the first time. Breathe slowly and deeply, remembering to breathe continuously and not to hold your breath. Communications are limited underwater, so watch for and follow your Instructor's hand signals.

Experiment with the effects of lung volume on buoyancy to begin learning how to use your lungs to your advantage underwater. Breathing shallowly with lungs nearly full makes you buoyant, and breathing shallowly with lungs nearly empty causes you to sink when you are properly weighted.

REGULATOR CLEARING

If you remove the regulator from your mouth underwater, the second stage will fill with water, but this is not a problem as the water can be easily cleared. The two standard methods for clearing a regulator are simply exhaling into it or using the purge button.

When removing the regulator from your mouth in the water, turn the mouthpiece downward. If turned upward, air may flow freely from the regulator and be wasted. Should free flowing occur, simply turn the mouthpiece downward.

The exhalation method of regulator clearing is as easy as it sounds. Simply blow into the regulator with the second stage in an upright position so the exhaust

The regulator may be cleared of water by momentarily depressing the purge button, or by simply exhaling into it before taking a breath

Develop the habit of exhaling slowly and continuously whenever the regulator is removed from your mouth

valve is the lowest point. Air inside the second stage will force all the water out through the exhaust. Remember that you must exhale before inhaling, and that the regulator must be in an upright position.

To use the purge button, place the second stage in your mouth and block the mouthpiece opening with your tongue to prevent water from being blown into your mouth and throat, then push the purge, which will admit air from the scuba tank, clearing the regulator and allowing you to take a breath.

The exhalation method of regulator clearing is the method almost always used. The purge button is for use when no air is available in the lungs to clear the regulator. Not having *any* air available from the lungs is unusual though, and only a small amount of air is needed to clear a regulator.

At this stage of training, begin to develop the habit of blowing a small, continuous stream of bubbles any time a regulator is not in your mouth while scuba diving. You must not hold your breath with compressed air in your lungs as you might forget, ascend, and cause lung damage due to overexpansion. By blowing bubbles, the airway to the lungs is kept open and expanding air can easily escape.

BREATHING WITHOUT A MASK

It is possible to have the mask flooded or dislodged underwater, so the ability to keep breathing while the nose is exposed to water is needed. With a little thought, concentration, and practice, you will be able to breathe easily through your mouth, while excluding water from your nose.

Breathing without a mask is a necessary skill which is not difficult to learn

At first it may be easier to inhale through your mouth and exhale through your nose. When this is comfortable, inhale and exhale through your mouth only. Should you feel any water entering your nose, just exhale slightly through the nose to keep the water out. With practice, breathing without a mask is as easy as breathing with one, and you will remain in complete control should your mask become flooded or dislodged.

Breathing without a mask

MASK CLEARING

Once you can breathe without a mask, clearing the mask of water will be easy. It is a matter of merely sealing the mask against your face, exhaling through the nose into the mask, and having the air force the water out at the lowest point. For a mask without a purge valve, hold the top of the mask tightly against the forehead and the bottom of the mask gently against the face, and look up while exhaling. (Be sure to begin exhaling before tipping the head back, or water will run into your nose.) If the mask has a purge valve, hold the mask snugly against the face and look down while exhaling to make the purge valve the lowest point.

To clear a mask without a purge valve, look up while exhaling.

Mask clearing is easiest when a steady, continuous exhalation is used. Before practicing mask clearing, learn to exhale an entire breath slowly and steadily through the nose. An easy way to do this is to hum. When clearing the mask, simply hum air into it until all the water has been displaced.

To clear a mask with a purge valve, make the valve the lowest point and hold the mask firmly against your face

When a mask is cleared properly, no air will escape: and since the volume of a mask is quite small compared to your lungs, a skilled diver can easily clear a mask four or five times with just a single breath of air.

SCUBA DESCENT

There are five points to be remembered in preparing for a scuba descent, and learning these points at the outset will make them easy to recall through repetition during training.

1. Your buddy should acknowledge agreement to descend.
2. Orient yourself to some surface object for reference.
3. Remove the snorkel from your mouth and replace it with the regulator mouthpiece. This can and should be done without lifting your head from the water. Remember to clear the regulator of water before taking a breath.
4. There is a need to note the time as there are time limitations for various depths in diving. You probably won't have an underwater watch during training, but should still look at your wrist just prior to descending to simulate checking the time of descent in order to develop a good diving habit.
5. The Buoyancy Control Device is deflated and you then exhale to initiate a

Scuba descent. Learn to descend feet first for control and orientation

feet-first descent, equalizing your ears immediately upon submerging and frequently during descent.

By controlling lung volume and the amount of air in the Buoyancy Control Device, and by keeping your fins beneath you during descent, you can maintain complete control and stop or ascend at any time.

SCUBA ASCENT

A five part plan of action is also used for ascending:

1. Your buddy should agree to ascend.
2. The time should be noted (or simulate by looking at your wrist).
3. One hand should be extended overhead for protection and the other hand on the BCD exhaust valve.
4. Look up and around during the entire ascent.
5. Swim up slowly while breathing normally. The correct rate of ascent is 60 feet per minute (one foot per second). An ascent from 30 feet, for example, requires 30 seconds.

SCUBA ENTRIES

In general, divers should ease into the water by wading or lowing themselves whenever possible. Some circumstances, however, require special entry techniques. Among the most commonly needed and used entries are the feet first entries.

When it is necessary to enter the water from a height of several feet, a feet first entry should be used. The BCD should be about one half inflated, all equipment should be in place the regulator mouthpiece should be in the mouth, and the mask should be held tightly in place. Be sure your buddy is ready to enter, check the area below, and simply step out with one foot. The back foot can then be pulled even with the front foot for a feet together entry, if the height is greater than 3-4 feet, or the legs can remain spread until contacting the water if the height is less. Pulling the legs together when hitting the water will keep you from going under as far as you will in a feet together entry.

Once in the water, swim clear of the entry area and wait for your buddy to enter.

Feet first entries.   Hold the mask firmly

Turn off the air

Purge the air remaining inside the regulator

DISASSEMBLY OF SCUBA EQUIPMENT

When finished using scuba, it is necessary to remove the regulator from the tank. To do this, the tank pressure on the yoke screw must be relieved. Turn off the air and purge the regulator before attempting to loosen the yoke screw. When removing the regulator, be careful not to allow any water to enter the high pressure inlet in the regulator first stage. After removing the regulator, thoroughly dry the regulator dust cover, position it over the high pressure inlet, and tighten the yoke screw to hold the dust cover snugly in place.

The back pack harness should not be left dangling after use. Wrap the straps around the pack and buckle them. This will keep the straps from dragging and tangling.

Be sure to dry and replace the dust cover

SECTION 3

- **The Diving Environment**
- **Diving Instruments**
- **Breathing Air at Depth**
- **More Scuba Skills**
- **Open Water Skills**

The Diving Environment

Environment is defined as the sum of all external conditions and influences affecting an organism. There are a number of diving conditions and influences which affect the diver, and these vary from day to day and from one area to another. Conditions are affected primarily by climate and weather. Diving techniques vary with the area, as do activities. An orientation, and perhaps training, are needed for diving in any new area, in unfamiliar conditions, or when engaging in a new activity.

GOALS

By the end of this module you should be able to:

1. Describe general environmental conditions affecting the diver, their effect on the diver, and how to cope with unfavorable effects.
2. Explain the importance of an orientation to a new diving area, condition, or activity.

*3. Recognize local hazards to avoid injury.

*4. Demonstrate familiarity with local laws and regulations pertaining to diving.

*This information will be presented by your Instructor during the classroom session.

GENERAL CONDITIONS

Temperature

Water temperatures range from 28°F in the Arctic to 85°F in the tropics. Within a given region temperatures usually vary less than 15°F throughout the year. Temperaure also changes with depth, generally getting colder as depth increases. A diver may also encounter a layer of colder water at depth. An abrupt transition to colder water at depth is called a thermocline, and is commonly encountered in fresh water lakes.

Loss of body heat to the water is the most significant effect and problem of water temperature. (See table on page 8.) Exposure suits are available to allow diving anywhere, but the proper type and amount of insulation must be used to prevent chilling. Diving in extremely cold or icy water requires special precautions and knowledge. Additional training is a necessity for diving in conditions of extreme cold.

Visibility

Visibility is defined as the horizontal distance underwater at which another diver can be clearly seen and ranges from zero to over 200 feet depending on the area and other conditions.

Some principle factors affecting visibility include water movement, weather, plankton or algae, and bottom composition. Waves, surf, and currents churn up sediment and reduce visibility. Muddy water from nearby land flowing into an area will reduce visibility after a rain. Microscopic animals (plankton) and plants (algae) become dense in the water under certain conditions and severely limit visibility. Red tides in the ocean, also called plankton blooms, kill animal life and give the water a reddish hue. Sediment on the bottom, disturbed by divers, boats, or water movement will billow up in clouds and quickly ruin visibility underwater.

Diving is done in water with limited visibility and . . .

in very clear water. Both require certain precautions.

Some effects of visibility are obvious, while others are subtle. With restricted visibility, it can be difficult to remain with your buddy, to determine where you are, and where you are going. Disorientation, particularly in mid-water (between the surface and the bottom), can result due to lack of reference. Use of a line for descents and ascents is recommended when visibility is limited. Navigation and buddy system techniques will help in coping with relative position and separation. When visibility is poor, avoid diving unless trained in limited visibility diving procedures.

You would not think extremely clear water could cause problems for the diver, yet it can. It is difficult to judge distances accurately, and very easy to go much deeper than planned. Disorientation can also occur in very clear water when no reference is available. Be aware of the possible effects of clear water, have accurate gauges, and refer to them frequently.

Currents

Surface and underwater currents are caused by tides, wind, waves, and bottom formations. They are mass movements of water and can be quite powerful. A diver working in or against a current can become fatigued or exhausted, unable to progress in a desired direction, and will use air at a faster rate.

It is important for divers to be able to recognize and estimate the local currents. Most divers cannot even make headway against a current as weak as one knot (1.15 mph), so they must learn to use currents to advantage or to avoid diving in them.

Divers generally begin dives against the current so it will help them return to their point of origin at the end of the dive. It is also easier to move against the current at the bottom, where the current is the least. If caught downstream in a current at the surface and unable to swim at the bottom,

DIVING IN CURRENTS

• START THE DIVE AGAINST THE CURRENT

swim across the current. You may be able to swim out of the current and then turn in the desired direction. Don't fight a strong current by swimming hard against it, as this leads to exhaustion. If caught in a current, establish buoyancy and signal for assistance, then wait for help or try to swim out of the current. Above all, remain calm. Most divers can swim at a leisurely pace for hours if positively buoyant.

There are special techniques for diving in currents and swift water. Be trained in these techniques before diving in conditions of strong water movement.

Water Density

The weight of a given quantity of water affects buoyancy. The denser the water, the more buoyancy provided for a given amount of water displaced. Salt water is denser than fresh water, so a diver will be more buoyant when diving in the ocean than when diving in a fresh water lake when using the same equipment. It is necessary to adjust the amount of weight used to be neutrally buoyant when diving in water of a different density.

Cold water is denser than warm water and will also slightly affect buoyancy. A thermocline can affect the buoyancy of a diver neutrally weighted for warmer surface water.

When you have determined the amount of weight needed for a certain diving situation, record the amount in your log book for future reference. Always check buoyancy at the beginning of any dive where the water density or the equipment used is different from normal.

Bottom Compositions

The composition of the bottom will affect the diver in several ways. Various compositions include silt, mud, sand, rock, coral, and vegetation. The most interesting diving areas are in rocks, coral, and vegetation. Besides affecting visibility, compositions may require precautions in entering and exiting and in moving about underwater. A diver may sink into a muddy bottom if trying to wade into the water. Objects dropped on a soft silt or sediment bottom can disappear from view. Entanglement in submerged trees, bushes, man made objects, or aquatic plants may occur if the diver is not cautious. Cuts and scrapes can occur from brushing against rocks and coral.

It is important to know the bottom composition of each dive site, any possible problems due to the composition, and how to cope with the problems.

Seek training for diving in any new environment

Animal and Plant Life

The vast majority of animals encountered underwater are harmless and timid. They either remain stationary or tend to flee at the presence of a diver. Very few are aggressive and these animals are seldom encountered. Injuries from animals are rare when compared with the number of dives made. Nearly all injuries are from defensive actions by an animal, not offensive, and generally result because the animal is frightened or threatened. Avoid either of these things and you'll rarely have any problems with animals. The most common injuries include puncture wounds from sea urchins, fish spines, and rays; stings from jellyfish and corals; and cuts and scrapes from rocks, barnacles, and coral. All of these injuries can be avoided. Learn to recognize and avoid potentially hazardous animals in the area where you dive. Wear protective clothing. Be neutrally buoyant, not heavy on the bottom, and move slowly. Look where you are going and where you place various parts of your body. If unfamiliar with an animal, leave it alone.

The mere sighting of an aggressive animal, such as a shark or barracuda, should not cause excessive alarm. Remain still and calm at the bottom, and watch the animal. These animals, particularly the barracuda, are not really the problem that Hollywood and the general populace would have you believe. If the animal makes return passes, move away from the area underwater and leave the water. Do not provoke attack by injuring the animal, wearing shiny objects, or carrying speared fish. Avoid diving in murky waters where aggressive animals are common. In most areas, problems from aggressive animals are so minimal as to be of no concern to experienced divers.

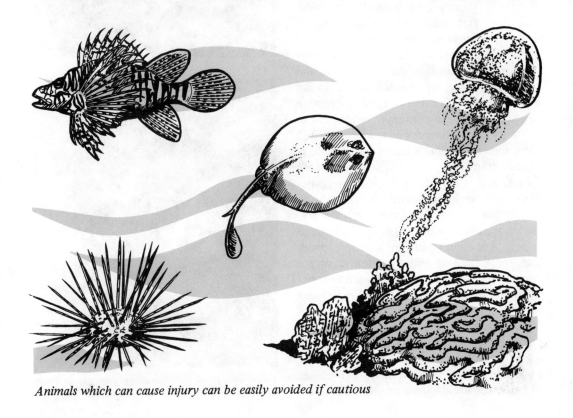

Animals which can cause injury can be easily avoided if cautious

Underwater hunting can be exciting and rewarding. Know and obey fish and game regulations.

Some animals are sought for food or specimens. Such animals include lobster, crab, abalone, scallops, fish, clams, conch, and other shellfish. Before taking any game, learn the local fish and game laws. Generally, there are seasons, sizes, limits, and other restrictions on game taken by divers. A license may be required. Fish and game laws are intended to assure a continuing supply of animals for future use and enjoyment. Obey all regulations, and take only what *you* can eat or use. Be reasonable in what you take to conserve for the future.

Plants provide cover and a source of food for numerous animals underwater. Life is abundant in areas where aquatic plants are found, and diving is very interesting because of the beauty and activity found among plants. The only concern when diving among plants is the possibility of entanglement, but even this is not a serious problem. With training and experience, divers can swim in and around plants without becoming entangled. Should entanglement occur, remain calm and work slowly to get free. Your buddy can help. Don't fight the entanglement. Pausing to think before taking action will be more effective than brute force. Streamlining equipment will reduce the chances of snagging or entanglement.

Underwater plants, such as the giant kelp, make dives interesting and beautiful.

Sunlight

The intensity of the sun's rays varies from one region to another, and divers should take precautions against sunburn. Prevention includes staying in the shade, protective clothing, and sun screening lotions. A cloudy day is no protection against sunburn, and sunburn is possible while in the water even though the diver feels cool. In tropical areas, light clothing worn while diving will provide protection. Be careful not to allow a dive trip or vacation to be ruined by overexposure to sunlight.

ENVIRONMENTAL OVERVIEW

There are two general diving environments — fresh water and salt water. Different conditions exist in each environment, and divers engage in different activities. A summary of general areas, activities, and precautions will help put diving in various regions into perspective, and will emphasize the need for regional orientations.

Fresh Water Diving

General diving areas in fresh water environments include lakes, quarries, springs, and rivers. Divers engage in general underwater activities, such as photography, bottle collecting, spearfishing, and artifact hunting, and also in specialty activities, including wreck diving, ice diving, cavern diving, and swift water diving. Each of

these specialties require special training and equipment. Be sure to obtain sanctioned training before diving in wrecks or caves, under the ice, or in rivers with strong currents. General problems to consider in the fresh water environment include currents, bottom compositions, limited visibility, thermoclines and cold water, entanglements, deep water, and boats. Diving may also take place at altitudes above sea level. For any dives at altitudes greater than 1,000 feet, special precautions must be observed, so additional training is necessary to learn safe techniques for diving at altitude.

Photo by Don Cook

Various fresh water and salt water diving locations

Salt Water Diving

Salt water diving is divided into three general areas — temperate, tropical, and arctic, with nearly all recreational diving occurring in the first two areas listed. Activities include all general underwater activities plus diving for game, shell collecting and diving from man made structures, such as jetties, piers, oil rigs, wrecks, and artificial reefs. General problems to consider in salt water include waves, surf, tides, currents, coral, boats, deep water, marine life, and remote locations.

It should be obvious by now that diving conditions and activities vary greatly from one area to another and that an orientation to an area or activity is quite important to assure diving safety.

OCEAN DIVING

The greatest amount of diving activity takes place in the oceans, and nearly all divers dive there at one time or another. Compared to fresh water, the ocean is very dynamic — constantly in motion. Familiarity with water movement in the ocean will be of value to all divers.

Other than offshore currents, nearly all the water movement of concern to the diver takes place in the surf zone. Waves, formed by wind blowing over the water, can travel thousands of miles until they encounter the shallow water of a beach. When the waves touch bottom, they slow down, peak up, become unstable, and break forward as surf, giving up their energy. The moving water in breaking waves can make entries and exits difficult for a diver unless special techniques are known and applied. Diving through the surf is a specialty and requires training.

As waves pass overhead in shallow water where they touch bottom, a back-and-forth movement of water, called surge, is felt by the diver. This surge can carry the diver some distance as large waves pass, and can be dangerous, especially in rocky areas. With small waves, the effect is not hazardous.

The size of waves is determined by the strength and duration of the wind forming them. Large waves, created by a strong wind blowing for many hours, can create unfavorable or hazardous diving conditions.

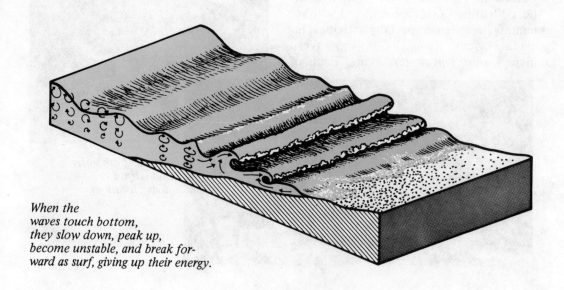

When the waves touch bottom, they slow down, peak up, become unstable, and break forward as surf, giving up their energy.

Waves building and breaking

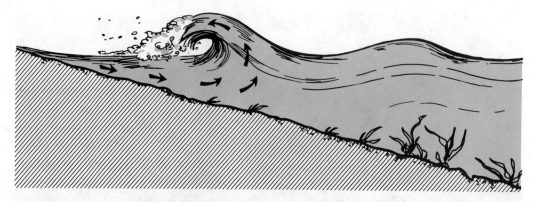

Backrush of a wave, sometimes called "undertow"

Divers and swimmers sometimes refer to the water flowing seaward after a wave rushes up on the beach as "undertow". This is actually the backrush of the wave, and dissipates at the depth no greater than three feet. There is no current which will pull objects under and sweep them out to sea. On steep beaches, the backrush can be quite strong when waves are large, and this can make exiting the water difficult.

Waves approaching shore break nearly parallel to it, but a slight angle exists between the shore and the surf, so water is pushed along the shoreline by the waves. This is called a longshore current and should be taken into consideration by a diver in order to avoid ending a dive downstream from the intended exit area.

Waves approaching shore at an angle push water along and cause a longshore current.

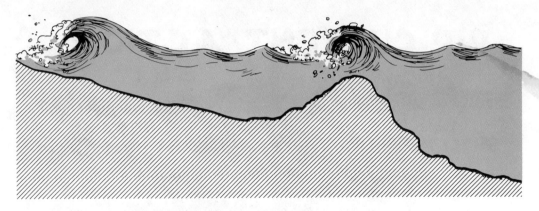

Waves breaking offshore indicate shallow water in the area.

Shallow water causes waves to break at a depth only slightly greater than the wave height. An offshore reef, wreck, or sand bar creating a shallow area can cause a wave to break, after which the wave will reform in deeper water, travel toward shore, and break again in shallow water. Waves breaking offshore indicate a shallow water area beneath.

At times waves may approach the shore from different directions. When this happens, the waves may run in sets — a series of larger waves followed by a series of smaller waves. This is caused by the waves approaching from different directions reinforcing or nullifying one another as their crests or troughs coincide.

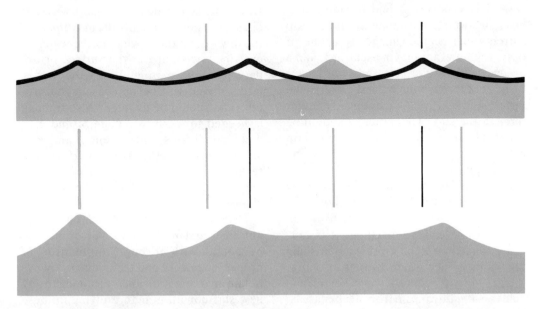

Wave patterns nullify or reinforce each other, resulting in periods of larger and smaller waves.

RIP CURRENT ACTION

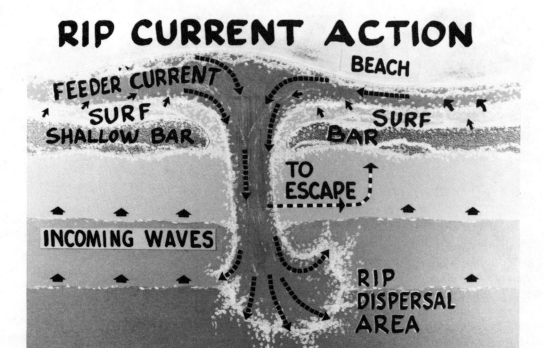

Another current which may occur in the surf zone is a rip current. This occurs when water piled up on the shore is funneled back to sea through a narrow opening such as a cut in a sand bar or reef. This type of current is very strong and alarming to a diver or swimmer unfamiliar with it. Rip currents can be recognized by a line of dirty, foamy water moving seaward, and a change in the wave pattern as the water rushes out through the waves. Divers who understand rips use them as an aid to enter through the surf. This practice should be avoided by inexperienced divers. If in a rip current while trying to return to shore and unable to make any progress, turn and swim parallel to the shore until clear of the rip area then turn back toward shore.

One other current of interest to ocean divers is one called upwelling. It is normally caused by an offshore wind pushing the warm surface water away from shore. This results in reduced wave height and colder water flowing up from deeper areas. This cold water is usually quite clear and contains nutrients which increase fish activity. Even though the water is colder, diving conditions are usually excellent following a period of upwelling.

All of this water movement in the surf zone affects the diver in many ways. It changes visibility, affects the movement of the diver at all times while in the water — entering, swimming at the surface or underwater, and exiting. When the surf is large, diving will be unpleasant, hazardous, and should be avoided. Also training is needed to learn to recognize and estimate conditions and to enter and exit safely through the surf. Surf diving techniques also vary from area to area, and even in the same area as the seasons change.

The surf zone can be dangerous to the untrained and inexperienced diver, but can be coped with through application of proper judgement and techniques. Always obtain an orientation and/or training to any new surf condition before diving in these areas.

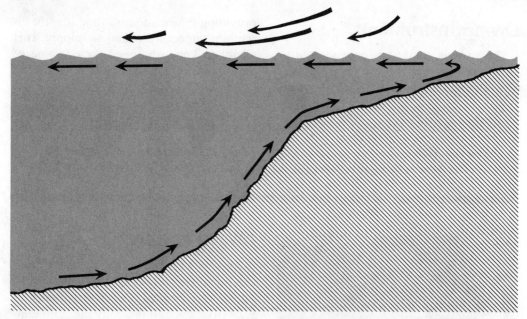

Upwelling, caused by wind blowing off-shore, often results in clear, colder water.

TIDES

Sea coasts have a rhythmic rise and fall of the water level. This variation in water level, called tide, is due to the gravitational pull of the moon and sun on the waters of the Earth. The time and height of tides vary considerably from place to place due to geographical location and configuration. The tides affect diving conditions because water movement is involved. Currents are produced, depth is changed, and visibility is changed by tides. Divers should consult local tide tables and learn the effects of tidal changes on diving in a particular area. Generally speaking, the best diving conditions occur at high tide.

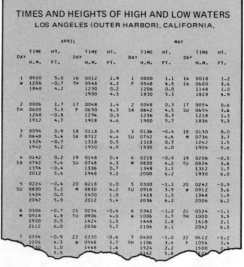

TIMES AND HEIGHTS OF HIGH AND LOW WATERS
LOS ANGELES (OUTER HARBOR), CALIFORNIA,

	APRIL							MAY				
DAY	TIME H.M.	HT. FT.	DAY	TIME H.M.	HT. FT.	DAY	TIME H.M.	HT. FT.	DAY	TIME H.M.	HT. FT.
1 W	0500	5.0	16 TH	0012	1.9	1 F	0000	1.1	16 SA	0018	1.2
	1206	-0.7		0548	4.2		0548	4.5		0600	3.6
	1848	4.2		1230	0.2		1206	0.0		1148	1.0
				1900	4.3		1830	5.3		1818	4.9
2 TH	0006	1.7	17 F	0048	1.4	2 SA	0048	0.3	17 SU	0054	0.6
	0600	5.3		0630	4.3		0642	4.5		0654	3.6
	1248	-0.8		1254	0.3		1236	0.3		1218	1.3
	1912	4.7		1918	4.6		1900	5.7		1836	5.3
3 F	0054	0.9	18 SA	0118	0.9	3 SU	0136	-0.4	18 M	0130	0.0
	0648	5.4		0712	4.4		0742	4.4		0736	3.7
	1324	-0.7		1318	0.5		1318	0.7		1242	1.5
	1942	5.2		1930	4.9		1930	6.0		1906	5.6
4 SA	0142	0.2	19 SU	0148	0.4	4 M	0218	-0.9	19 TU	0206	-0.5
	0742	5.4		0748	4.3		0830	4.2		0824	3.6
	1354	-0.4		1336	0.7		1348	1.1		1312	1.7
	2012	5.6		1948	5.2		2000	6.2		1930	6.0
5 SU	0224	-0.4	20 M	0218	0.0	5 TU	0300	-1.1	20 W	0242	-0.9
	0830	5.2		0830	4.2		0918	3.9		0912	3.6
	1424	0.0		1400	1.0		1418	1.5		1348	2.1
	2042	5.9		2012	5.4		2036	6.2		2006	6.2
6 M	0306	-0.7	21 TU	0254	-0.4	6 W	0342	-1.2	21 TH	0324	-1.1
	0918	4.8		0906	4.0		1006	3.7		1000	3.5
	1500	0.5		1424	1.3		1448	1.8		1418	2.1
	2112	6.0		2036	5.7		2106	6.1		2042	6.3
7	0354	-0.9	22 W	0330	-0.6	7 TH	0430	-1.0	22 F	0412	-1.2
	1006	4.3		0948	3.7		1106	3.4		1054	3.4
	30	1.0		1448	1.6		1524	2.2		1500	2.1
		5.9					2142	5.8			

Tide Tables

SUMMARY

There are many environmental conditions affecting the diver, and the conditions vary somewhat from one dive site to another and often radically from one region to another. Divers need to know the effects of various conditions on diving, and exercise good judgment in evaluating the diving conditions. If conditions are poor, or if you are uncertain about your ability to handle the situation, don't make the dive. Seek orientation or training to any new environmental situation.

Diving Instruments

The various conditions encountered in diving create a need for reference information. Diving instruments fulfill this need, providing information on time, depth, direction, temperature, and air supply. It is useful to know the need for or value of various instruments for general diving.

GOALS

By the end of this module, you should be able to explain the need for a watch, depth gauge, compass, and thermometer, and the fundamental use of these instruments for diving.

A diving watch. Set the dial to indicate the beginning of a dive . . .

and the elapsed time will be indicated on the dial as shown.

DIVING WATCH

There are limits of time at which a diver can remain at various depths. If these time limits are exceeded, the diver will absorb excessive gas into the body due to the increased pressure at depth. It is necessary, therefore, to keep track accurately of the time spent underwater. A variety of waterproof diving watches are available for this purpose. A common diving watch feature is a rotating bezel (dial) which can be aligned with the minute hand at the start of the dive and allows the dive time to be read directly at the end of the dive.

A dive watch should be treated with care, rinsed after each dive, removed when bathing, and cleaned and lubricated annually.

DEPTH GAUGE

A depth gauge is considered a necessary item of diving equipment. The length of time permitted on a dive is dependent upon the depth at which the dive will occur. A depth gauge is also needed for reference to make certain the depth limit is not exceeded during successive dives on the same day.

There are various types of gauges available at a wide range of prices. Generally, the inexpensive gauges are quite satisfac-

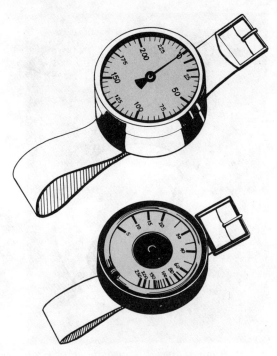

Depth gauges

tory for shallow depths, while the more expensive gauges are required for accuracy at deeper depths.

Treat depth gauges with care and rinse them after use. Follow the manufacturer's instructions. Mechanical gauges can be damaged by reduced pressure at altitude, so they should be kept in an airtight container when flying or going high into the mountains.

COMPASS

A compass is a navigational aid — a reference tool for the diver. It allows you to know your direction in relation to where the dive started or will end, and is useful for following a designated course. A compass is a necessary item in turbid water, where surface fog can prevent visual reference, and when diving at night.

A diving compass is liquid filled and unaffected by pressure. The preferred type of compass will have a reference line, called the lubber line, and index markers which can be aligned over the compass needle to indicate a directional heading. Use of the compass is presented in the skills portion of this section.

THERMOMETER

A thermometer is not an essential diving instrument, but does provide useful information for the diver about water temperature. This information is helpful in keeping records of water conditions, planning future dives, and as a general reference. There are several types of underwater thermometers available on the market.

SUBMERSIBLE PRESSURE GAUGE

The SPG provides information on the amount of air remaining in the tank and was previously discussed (refer to page 69). It is a standard item of equipment and mandatory on all scuba dives.

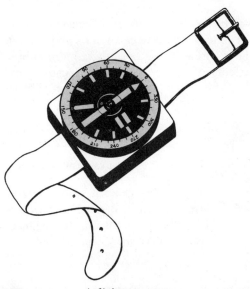

A diving compass

INSTRUMENT PANEL

Various panels are available which attach to the submersible pressure gauge and allow a number of diving instruments to be attached. This removes the gauges from the wrists and consolidates them in one location for ease of use. An instrument panel is an accessory item intended for convenience in use of diving instruments.

SUMMARY

Having reference information available while diving helps a diver plan, make correct decisions, and dive safely. Without instruments, a diver can become disoriented and exceed safe limits. Diving instruments provide needed information. Some instruments are considered standard equipment, and depending on conditions and location, others may be required.

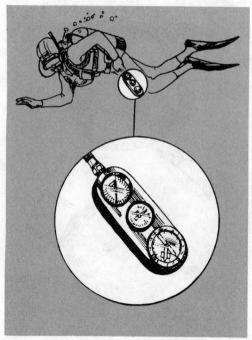

An instrument panel consolidates various gauges.

Breathing Air at Depth

The mechanical effects of pressure, such as squeezes, are very obvious and cannot be ignored. There are other, more subtle effects of pressure, however, caused by breathing gases under pressure. These gases can have profound effects upon divers. These effects are predictable, understood, and can be controlled by following recommended guidelines. A knowledge of the effects of various common gases breathed under pressure, the symptoms of resultant abnormalities, and how to avoid these problems is needed.

THE AIR WE BREATHE

Your tank should be filled by a reputable air station with pure, dry, filtered compressed air — essentially a mixture of nitrogen and oxygen. (See Air Purity Standards in the Appendix). While these gases have no adverse effects at atmospheric pressure, both can produce hazardous situations when breathed under high pressures. Oxygen creates problems only when present in very large quantities, so nitrogen is the gas of primary concern at increased pressures. Nitrogen is physiologically inert, but imposes limits on time and depth as it is absorbed into the body under higher than normal pressures. Air can also be contaminated with other gases. To prevent contamination, an air station usually takes special precautions and has their air periodically tested. The toxicity of contaminants increases as the pressure increases, so the effects and symptoms should be known in order to prevent serious difficulties underwater.

CONTAMINATED AIR

If a compressor is not set up, operated, and maintained properly, contaminants can be introduced into scuba tanks. Thus it is important to obtain your air from a reputable, professional air station.

Contaminated air will generally taste and smell foul, or cause headaches, nausea, or dizziness when breathed. The contaminants can be odorless and tasteless, however, and unconsciousness can occur without warning. A diver afflicted by contaminated air will have cherry red lips and nail beds.

A person suffering from contaminated air poisoning should have fresh air and oxygen should be administered if available. Artificial respiration may be required. Medical attention is needed even in cases that are not severe. Save remaining air for analysis.

To prevent poisoning from contaminated air, do not use air that tastes or smells unusual. Surface and abort a dive if

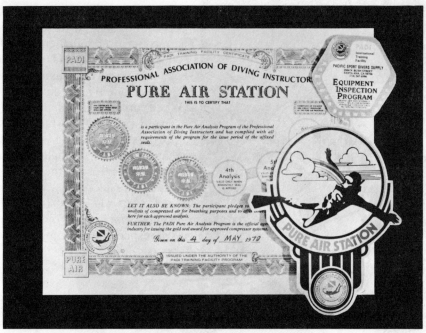

Look for these symbols of air purity.

you feel ill while underwater, and obtain air only from a reliable source. Because the effects of air contamination are serious, those who operate compressors are conscientious, so poisoning from contaminated scuba air is relatively rare in diving. However, contaminated air poisoning is possible from breathing exhaust fumes aboard a boat, so use caution.

OXYGEN

Pure oxygen under pressure is toxic and will lead to severe disorders. Since air contains only 20% oxygen, there is no danger from the oxygen contained in it except at extreme depths — far beyond the 100 feet sport diving limit. If a scuba tank were to be filled with oxygen, however, instead of compressed air, oxygen toxicity would occur at shallow depths. Fill scuba tanks with compressed air only.

 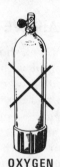

COMPRESSED AIR   OXYGEN

Fill scuba tanks with compressed air only.

NITROGEN NARCOSIS

Adverse effects from oxygen and contaminated air are uncommon in sport diving, but the effects of nitrogen need to be considered on every dive. Breathing compressed air at depths approaching 100 feet can produce a narcotic effect similar to that resulting from breathing anesthetic gases. Some individuals are more susceptible to nitrogen narcosis than others. Individual effects vary from day to day, and the effects become more pronounced with increasing depth or stenuous activity.

Symptoms of nitrogen narcosis are like those of intoxication in several respects. There is impaired judgment and skill, lack of concern for safety, and foolish behavior. These effects can be disastrous due to poor decisions made by the diver.

When narcosis occurs, the diver may not be aware of it unless familiar with the symptoms. If feeling strangely, immediately ascend to shallower depths to determine if narcosis is the problem. Relief will usually result quickly and there are no after effects from narcosis, which can be prevented simply by avoiding deep dives. This is especially true for inexperienced divers.

Deep dives can cause nitrogen narcosis and unsafe behavior.

DECOMPRESSION SICKNESS

Perhaps the single greatest effect of breathing air under pressure is the absorption of nitrogen into body tissues due to increased pressure. The longer a diver remains underwater and the greater the depth, the more nitrogen is absorbed. When the pressure is reduced during ascent, this nitrogen must be slowly eliminated through respiration or bubbles will form in the bloodstream and cause a serious illness commonly known as the bends.

A diver can tolerate a limited amount of excess nitrogen in the system. Special tables have been developed by the Navy which establish time and depth limits and an ascent rate to keep nitrogen levels within acceptable bounds. Exceeding the table limits can result in localized pain, itching of the skin, or difficulty in breathing. In severe cases, paralysis, unconsciousness, and even death can result. Other factors contribute to the uptake and elimination of nitrogen and can lead to decompression sickness. These factors include fatigue, cold, age, illness, and being overweight. Sport divers should dive well within established limits and use caution if any contributing factors are involved.

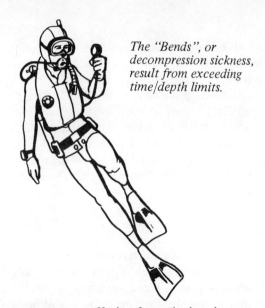

The "Bends", or decompression sickness, result from exceeding time/depth limits.

A person suffering from the bends must be placed under pressure, or recompressed, to relieve the symptoms. This must be done in a chamber filled with compressed air, called a recompression chamber. Trying to recompress a diver underwater can compound the injury and create additional problems of exposure and logistics. A bends victim should be treated for shock, given oxygen if available, and transported to the nearest recompression chamber. Artificial respiration may be necessary if the victim has breathing difficulties.

Recompression chamber

When divers absorb excessive nitrogen, they must ascend to a designated depth to reduce the pressure and remain there for a specified period of time to allow sufficient elimination of nitrogen before surfacing. This is called decompression diving and is beyond the scope of recreational diving. Sport divers should always dive within established no-decompression limits on all dives.

Since the reduction of pressure can cause bubble formation, it is easy to see how a further reduction of pressure below sea level pressure can result in decompression sickness which would not normally occur, or in a more severe case of the bends. Air pressure decreases as altitude increases, so traveling at altitudes after diving can cause or worsen decompression sickness. The procedure for flying after diving will be explained along with the use of the decompression tables in Section Four.

The Navy decompression tables are inaccurate for diving above sea level. Diving at altitudes above 1,000 feet is a specialty requiring additional training.

DECOMPRESSION METER

Special tables are used in conjunction with a watch and depth gauge to determine the limits of time and depth for dives. Use of these items is complicated and requires frequent practice for accuracy in planning and execution. To deal with these difficulties, meters have been designed to automatically take all the necessary factors into consideration and provide a visual readout to inform the diver of the limits. This concept is sound and such devices are acceptable provided they have been proven accurate and reliable, are used within their capabilities and according to the manufacturer's instructions, and are periodically tested and calibrated. Even when a reliable meter is used, underwater time and depth should be noted as a check against the tables recommendations. A meter should be used only when the dive tables are used — never instead of the tables.

SUMMARY

The air you breathe should not cause problems in diving if recommended procedures and guidelines are followed. Obtain air from a reputable air station, do not make deep dives, and consult the decompression tables for the time limits at various depths. Divers ignoring or violating these rules are jeopardizing their safety instead of assuring enjoyment. Safe diving is fun diving.

Decreased pressure at altitudes above sea level can cause decompresson sickness unless special diving procedures are followed.

More Scuba Skills

Previously learned skin and scuba diving skills have prepared you to learn more complex scuba skills needed for open water diving. You can now handle the weight belt and scuba unit out of the water, but need to learn to handle them in the water as well. Also, you need to learn to use the Buoyancy Control Device to control buoyancy underwater. In this session you will also learn how to share air and to exit from water deeper than your height.

GOALS

Your goal is to be able to perform the following skills properly and easily by the end of the third Skill Development Session:

1. Removal and replacement of the weight belt underwater.
2. Removal and replacement of the weight belt at the surface.
3. Removal and replacement of the scuba unit underwater.
4. Removal and replacement of the scuba unit at the surface.
5. Oral inflation of the Buoyancy Control Device Underwater.
6. Adjustment of buoyancy to achieve neutral buoyancy underwater.
7. Buddy Breathing.
8. Deep water exit.

WEIGHT BELT HANDLING

You may have occasion to remove or replace the weight belt in the water while diving. By following certain procedures, this can be accomplished easily. The two primary points to remember are, (1) to hold the belt by the free end (the end without the buckle) to keep the weights from sliding off, and (2) to work with the belt while lying horizontally in a facedown position with the belt draped across your back. These points apply both at the surface and underwater.

When removing the weight belt, pull it clear of the body. Simply releasing the buckle will not assure the belt will be jettisoned as it may catch on various items. If you intend to hold the belt after removal, keep it close to you, as holding it away from the body tends to pull you over in the

When ditching the weight belt, pull it clear before releasing it.

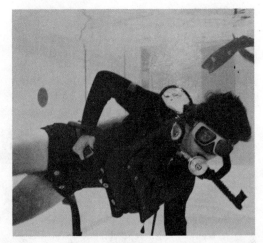

To reposition the weight belt, hold the free end against your right hip and roll the belt into place across your back.

water. The best method for replacing a belt after removal is to position yourself in a horizontal face-up position and hold the weight nearest the free end against your right hip, then roll to the left to a facedown position so the belt goes automatically into position across the small of your back. When wearing scuba, it may be necessary to arch the back forward slightly to get the belt under the end of the tank. Once the belt is positioned, lying facedown will relieve any strain on the buckle, and the belt can be tighted and secured without difficulty. Learn to fasten the buckle by feel rather than by sight because it is difficult or impossible to see the bukcle when wearing a mask and BCD in the water.

SCUBA TANK HANDLING

You may also need to don your scuba tank while in the water, or, should entanglement occur, to remove and replace it underwater. As in weight belt handling, there are techniques to make this skill easy to accomplish.

Handling the tank in the water is easy, as it is nearly weightless. Removal is as easy as taking off a coat. The only problems

occur when putting on the unit, and these can be avoided with familiarization and skill development.

To replace the scuba unit, position it in front of you with the valve toward you and the backpack facing upward. Be sure the shoulder strap quick release is fastened and the straps are adjusted to the approximate size needed. Place each arm through the shoulder straps past the elbow, being careful the regulator hose is between your arms. The hose must go directly from the tank to you without going around your arm or it will be trapped when the unit is donned. The next step is to exhale to reduce buoyancy, and to raise the unit up and over your head, lowering it into place on your back. Be careful the snorkel does not get caught when the tank passes overhead. Also be sure the BCD collar and inflator hose are not caught under the straps after lowering the unit into place. Reach back and grasp the waist straps to pull the unit into place, make any needed adjustments, then fasten the waist strap. This procedure works well both at the surface and underwater. The only difference is to have the BCD partially inflated at the surface to provide positive buoyancy.

To don the scuba tank in the water, place arms through straps past the elbows and be sure the regulator hose is between the arms.

Raise the tank up and over the head.

Lower the tank into place.

Be sure the BCD collar and inflator hose are clear before securing the tank.

USING THE BCD UNDERWATER

When descending in open water, it will be necessary to add air to the BCD to compensate for changes in buoyancy at depth. When ascending, this additional air will expand and create excessive buoyancy unless it is expelled from the BCD, resulting in an ascent which is too rapid. The following procedures briefly describe how to inflate the BCD underwater, how to determine neutral buoyancy at depth, and how to control buoyancy during ascent.

To orally inflate the BCD underwater, grasp the regulator second stage in the right hand and the BCD inflator in the left

When inflating the BCD underwater, save some air in your lungs for clearing the regulator.

With proper buoyancy, you should be able to pivot on your fin tips, rising when slowly inhaling, and sinking when exhaling.

hand, take a breath, remove the regulator from your mouth, and exhale about two thirds of your air into the BCD (save enough air to clear the regulator). Repeat until sufficient buoyancy is achieved.

Estimating neutral buoyancy underwater will be easy with experience, but it can be somewhat difficult at first. Movement occurs slowly in water, so changes in buoyancy will not result in an immediate up or down movement. It takes a few seconds for this to happen, so wait for the results before making further changes in the amount of air in the BCD. A good method to achieve neutral buoyancy underwater is to lay facedown on the bottom and breathe slowly and deeply, then add air to the BCD until you pivot slightly upward on the tips of your fins as you inhale and pivot downward when you exhale. At this point you will be neutrally buoyant.

Remember that a change in depth results in a change in the volume of air in the BCD and a resultant change in buoyancy. Buoyancy control is more critical at shallow depths, as a result of a more rapid expansion of air in shallow water. You will

need to adjust buoyancy with changes in depth. You may forget this at first and find yourself floating away from the bottom when you don't intend to ascend. To overcome this, exhale, swim downward, locate the deflator and expel air from the BCD, then establish neutral buoyancy. If you are unable to do this, and a runaway ascent occurs due to excessive buoyancy, assume a spread eagle position in the water to create the maximum resistance to movement. Breathe continuously and maintain a normal lung volume during the ascent. Uncontrolled ascents do not occur to experienced, aware divers.

During a normal controlled ascent, the deflator should be held in one hand throughout the ascent, and small amounts of air expelled from time to time to prevent excessive buoyancy. The objective is to maintain neutral buoyancy throughout the ascent as the air in the BCD expands. Upon surfacing, the BCD should immediately be inflated to establish positive buoyancy. This is one of a number of skills which should receive conscious attention while being practiced repeatedly until it becomes automatic and is done without thinking.

Hold the BCD inflator in one hand during ascent and expel air as needed to prevent excessive buoyancy.

*Buddy Breathing.
Divers hold onto each
other for coordination
and stability. Exhale
whenever the regulator
is not in your mouth.*

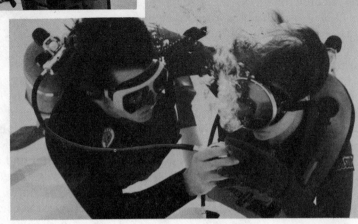

*Sharing air while swimming.
Notice the receiver of air
grasping the regulator to
guide it into her mouth.*

BUDDY BREATHING

This skill is the sharing of a single supply of air in the event that one diver of a team experiences an abrupt termination of air supply underwater. It is simply a matter of passing the regulator mouthpiece back and forth between divers with each diver taking two breaths at a time. Buddy breathing is less desirable than using an octopus attachment, but needs to be learned in case a need to share air exists and an extra second stage is not available.

Buddy breathing is initiated with the signals "out of air" and "give me air". At this time, the diver with air holds the regulator in the right hand and extends it toward the diver needing air. With the left hand, the diver with air holds the receiver to prevent separation. The receiver of air holds onto the buddy with the right hand and uses the left hand to help guide the regulator mouthpiece into the mouth. The diver with air maintains possession and control of the mouthpiece at all times and does not release it to the receiver. It is important not to hold your breath during buddy breathing. Any time the regulator is not in your mouth, exhale a small, steady, continuous stream of bubbles.

The face-to-face position for buddy breathing is shown in the illustration. In this position the divers can remain stationary or can swim upwards. By assuming the same position parallel with the bottom, it is possible to practice buddy breathing while swimming horizontally underwater.

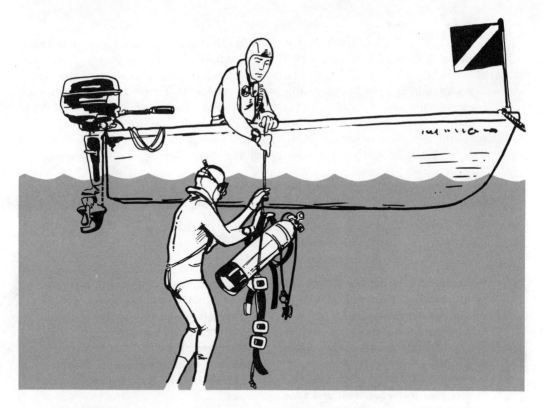

It is often helpful to remove the scuba tank and weight belt before exiting the water.

DEEP WATER EXIT

At times it may be necessary to remove scuba, weight belt and fins to exit the water. This skill needs to be developed under controlled conditions before being applied in open water situations.

The BCD should be partially inflated to provide positive buoyancy. The weight belt should then be removed and attached to a line or removed from the water. The scuba unit is then handled similarly. Fins should be removed last, only if necessary, and only while maintaining contact with the exit point. If waves are present, time them to assist you in exiting. Try to exit when the waves will help lift you onto the platform, boat, rocks, etc.

Open Water Skills

Some diving skills need to be developed at actual dive sites. These skills cannot be learned in a swimming pool, as the water isn't deep enough or distances great enough, and the water conditions are not like those of the actual environment. More equipment is generally needed for open water diving than is used in pool training. Entry and exit techniques vary with each situation. It is necessary to learn under supervision to handle yourself and your equipment, and to apply various skills in the open water environment under conditions similar to those in which you'll be diving after training.

GOALS

Your goal is to be able to perform the following open water skills properly and easily by the end of the course:

1. Estimate local diving conditions and make a reasonable determination as to whether or not the conditions are safe and appropriate for diving.
2. Suit up efficiently for open water diving and without overexerting or becoming overheated.
3. Inspect your own equipment and your buddy's for any malfunctions or misadjustments prior to entering the water for a dive.
4. Safely enter and exit the water independently using techniques appropriate for local diving situations.
5. Distance swim at the surface using the snorkel while wearing scuba without overexerting and while maintaining a set course and buddy contact.
6. Free descend feet first using buoyancy control, maintaining neutral buoyancy and buddy contact, and with no discomfort.
7. Set and follow a compass heading underwater for at least 50 yards.
8. Use a compass for reference during a dive in which direction is changed several times, knowing continuously your position relative to the starting point.

EVALUATING CONDITIONS

You need to be able to estimate diving conditions at the dive site and to determine if the physical requirements for a dive are within your capabilities. Your Instructor will show you how to evaluate such considerations as current, visibility, wave action, and area hazards. You should also learn sources of information about weather, depth, water temperature, bottom composition and contour, and other factors. It is important to select entry and exit points prior to the dive and to determine the entry and exit procedures. Your evaluation and determinations should be done upon arrival at the dive site and before suiting up. Decide whether or not you can make the dive safely. If you or your buddy do not feel confident to handle the situation, do something else that's enjoyable, as diving in poor or hazardous conditions is not fun, and enjoyment, not danger, is what you should seek from diving.

Evaluate conditions upon arrival at the dive site.

SUITING UP

Diving is an equipment oriented sport and putting on all of the necessary gear for scuba diving can be a problem. You can become frustrated, overheated, tired, and breathless unless you handle the procedure properly. Your goal is to suit up at the same time as your buddy and enter the water rested. To achieve this, check and adjust all your equipment in advance. Organize your gear in the order in which it will be put on. When suiting up, take your time, work steadily, and rest occasionally. Pace yourself with your buddy and help each other, but try to be independent as much as possible to become familiar with your gear and to develop self-reliance. Most scuba divers put their gear on in the following sequence:

1. Pants and boots. (Tuck boots under pants legs)
2. Hood and jacket.
3. Buoyancy Control Device. (Straps previously adjusted)
4. Cool off in water as needed to prevent overheating.

Work as a team so you and your buddy will be suited up at the same time.

5. Scuba and weight belt. (Harness and belt previously adjusted)
6. Mask and snorkel. (Strap and snorkel previously adjusted)
7. Fins and gloves. (Fin straps previously adjusted)

Suiting up may seem troublesome at first, but when you have your own gear and are experienced with it, the task will become an easy one.

EQUIPMENT INSPECTION

After suiting up and before entering the water, you should check your own equipment for adjustment and function, and should also inspect your buddy's gear. Buddies should face each other and check for the following:

1. Buoyancy Control Device snugly adjusted and clear of tank harness.
2. Buoyancy Control Device operability. (Check mechanical inflator and oral inflator.)
3. Weight belt is over all other gear and clear for ditching.
4. Familiarity with location and operation of buddy's equipment releases.

Be familiar with the location and operation of your buddy's equipment.

A sitting back entry is used when entering the water from a low, unstable platform, such as a small boat.

5. Air supply. Diver A turns around, and Diver B checks Diver A's air supply. (Air on, regulator functioning, tank pressure, reserve position, and hoses clear.) Diver B should also determine how to locate and obtain the extra second stage on Diver A.
6. Both divers turn around and Diver A checks Diver B's air supply.
7. Each receives final OK from buddy after overall inspection. (No dangling straps, trapped hoses, or missing gear.)

This inspection procedure should be memorized and conducted before every dive. It can be remembered very simply with the following phrase:

1. Buoyancy Control Device — Begin
2. Weight Belt — With
3. Releases — Review
4. Air Supply — And
5. Final OK — Friend

OPEN WATER ENTRIES — GENERAL

Review the general entry techniques on page 36. With some exceptions, the following additional practices are recommended for scuba entries where the diver walks into the water:

1. Put on your fins at the water's edge before entering. Have all equipment in place.

2. Breathe from scuba during the entry until you are in deep water and have control.

3. Walk backwards or sideways and shuffle your feet. This detects holes and obstructions, reduces the chance of falling, and chases away bottom dwelling creatures which might injure you if stepped upon.

4. Get horizontal in the water and start swimming as soon as the water is deep enough.

Entry techniques vary with locations and situations. You will learn the proper methods for the local training sites, but these will not be applicable for all situations. An orientation to diving in a new area should include entry and exit techniques.

Hold your masks and steady each other as you back into the water.

*Hold masks,
have regulators in place,
and keep knees bent
during surf entries.*

OPEN WATER ENTRIES — SURF

Surf entries require special training, however, you could enter through mild surf on a smooth beach by applying a few simple procedures. Breathing from your regulator, back into the water while looking continuously over your shoulder to watch incoming waves. Look over the shoulder on the side facing your buddy so you can keep track of him or her. Keep your knees bent, stop when the wave is about to meet you, and lean slightly into the wave to offset its force; then start moving again after it has passed. Keep one hand on your mask continually. As soon as the water is deep enough, lay down and start swimming, allowing waves to pass over you until clear of the surf zone. Keep holding the mask until beyond the breaking waves. Swim steadily, and don't stop in the surf zone. When clear of the surf zone,

come upright, check your buddy, get together and rest before proceeding. The entire surf entry should take less than a minute with not more than two or three waves passing over you. If a surface float is being used, tow it behind. If unfamiliar or unsure about the entry, make a practice entry first without scuba or weight belt.

Surf entries require training and practice.

SURFACE SWIMMING

In open water, surface swimming presents problems not faced in a pool. These are due in part to visibility, distance, and water movement. Problems such as overexertion and separation from your buddy can be avoided by following some simple recommendations.

1. Have your BCD about 50% inflated.
2. Pace yourself. Proceed at a steady, comfortable pace.
3. Extend hands in front or trail them at your side. Streamline yourself to reduce resistance to motion.

Surface swimming in open water

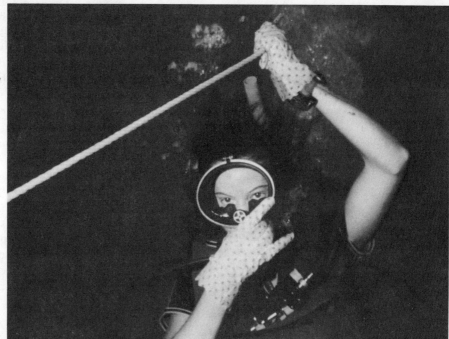

Controlled descent

4. Breathe in cautiously to avoid choking on water which may enter the snorkel due to surface chop.
5. Keep fins below the water surface when kicking. Kick downward more than up.
6. Lift your head momentarily at least every 30 seconds to check your direction and your buddy's location. Use a distant object as a guide to keep on course. Maintain physical contact with buddy if visibility is limited.

DESCENDING

Open water descents require extra considerations compared to pool descents due to greater depth and sediment on the bottom. Scuba divers should descend feet first in order to maintain control, buddy contact, and orientation. After deflating the BCD, a properly weighted diver can initiate the descent with a complete exhalation, breathing shallowly until a loss of buoyancy occurs. Remember to equalize pressure in air spaces early and often. Maintain neutral buoyancy during the descent, using breath control and the BCD. On dives below 30 feet, it will be necessary to add air to the BCD during descent. Finning should be kept to minimum, with control being maintained with buoyancy. Kicking your fins as you approach the bottom will stir up clouds of sediment and reduce or eliminate visibility.

Initial descents should be made on a line for control and reference. If an anchorline is used, be alert for hazardous movement of the line caused by the motion of the boat at the surface. Hold the line at arm's length.

When controlled descents can be easily accomplished, the ability to make a free descent with no line or reference should be developed.

A diver should be able to descend steadily and easily, maintaining neutral buoyancy so the ascent can be stopped at any time, while maintaining buddy contact and a sense of direction.

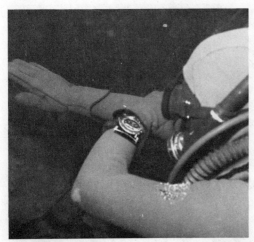

Look over the compass rather than down on it for navigating.

BASIC COMPASS NAVIGATION

With vision limited, travelling underwater is similar to making your way without references through a dense fog above water. Loss of a sense of direction occurs easily, but a compass can provide a reference to cope with the problem in either situation. A compass is a suspended needle which is magnetically attracted to the North pole, allowing you to determine your direction in relation to North.

An underwater compass should have a reference line, or "lubber line", through its center. To use the compass, simply point the lubber line in the direction you desire to travel, note the heading, and keep the needle pointed at that heading. Some compasses have a bezel with index marks which can be aligned over the needle to provide a reference. There is then no need to recall the heading; simply keep the needle within the index marks and you will be on course.

When following a heading, it is important to keep the compass level and the lubber line of the compass in line with the centerline of your body. The recommended method to do this is to use the position shown in the illustration.

When changing course, right angle turns are recommended, as this makes it easy to determine your direction relative to your initial heading. One turn would change your heading by 90°, and another turn in the same direction would change it by another 90°, resulting in a reciprocal course — one taking you back toward your starting point. Again, using index marks simplifies use of the instrument. Leave the index marks set at their initial heading, then note the needle direction relative to their position.

The compass is a simple device, not difficult to learn to use, but its importance in all but the clearest waters cannot be overemphasized. Proper use of the compass makes diving easier and more enjoyable.

Keep the compass in line with the body for accuracy in navigation.

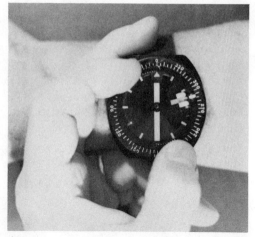

To set a compass heading, aim the compass in the desired direction and align the index marks over the needle.

SURF EXITS

If you entered through the surf, you will probably also exit there! Here are some guidelines for surf exits:

1. Save some air for the exit. You should have 300 to 500 psi left at the end of every dive. It is easier to breathe from scuba in the moving water and using the regulator keeps it from getting clogged with sand.

2. Stop just outside the surf zone to evaluate the situation. Catch your breath and discuss the exit with your buddy before starting in.

3. Hold your mask constantly in the surf zone. Keep your free hand extended in front of you.

4. Stay apart from and abreast of your buddy. Avoid being behind another diver in the surf zone.

5. Swim steadily toward shore and into knee deep water before standing. If the backrush is strong, swim all the way to shore and crawl out on all fours for greater stability.

6. Check on your buddy between waves.

7. Keep all gear in place until clear of the water. Don't stop in the surf zone.

8. If a surface float is used, push it ahead during the exit. Do not ride the float.

In surf it is often easier to swim all the way to shore and crawl out of the water than it is to stand and try to walk.

SECTION

- **Accessory Diving Equipment**
- **Health For Diving**
- **Dive Planning**
- **Dive Tables Introduction**
- **Diving Emergencies**
- **More Scuba Skills**

Accessory Diving Equipment

In addition to the standard equipment needed for diving, numerous accessory items are available to fill various needs. The most commonly used accessories will be presented here. You will be introduced to many more as your diving experience increases.

GOALS

By the end of this module, you should be able to describe and explain the purpose of commonly used diving accessory items.

SURFACE FLOATS

Surf mats, rubber rafts, and inner tubes are examples of surface floats used for diving. These floats are especially useful for shore entry dives as they can be used for equipment storage, resting stations, dive

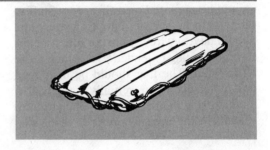

Different types of diver's floats commonly used.

The diver's flag warns boaters of diving activities.

flag support, or rescue assistance. Surface floats are anchored with small anchors or towed by divers throughout the dive. This means they will usually have fifty or so feet of line attached to them. Divers should take caution to avoid entanglement in the line and should use a holder of some type to keep the excess line from drifting loose in the water. The line should not be tied to the diver.

DIVE FLAG

The dive flag is an important safety device to warn boaters of divers in the area — to be alert for the divers and to stay clear. The flag, which is required in some states, is square or rectangular and red with a white diagonal stripe, and should be visible in the water from a distance of at least 100 yards. To aid in making the flag visible, it should be mounted on a three foot staff to allow it to be seen in choppy water, and should have a wire support or other means to hold the flag extended even when there is no wind. The flag should be displayed only when divers are actually in the water. Divers using the flag have an obligation to remain in the area where it is being displayed.

COLLECTING BAGS

Various types and sizes of bags are available to hold and contain assorted objects, such as equipment, game, or artifacts. Collecting bags are often referred to as goodie bags or game bags. Different types have various features. Generally, collecting bags have a means for water to drain from them rapidly, and a wire frame to hold the top open widely or closed and locked securely. For safety, collecting bags should be carried by hand rather than being attached to the weight belt.

Collecting bags

UNDERWATER LIGHTS

Besides being a must for diving at night, underwater lights are useful for looking under ledges, into holes, and to view underwater objects in their full, true colors. A wide range of lights are available, with various sizes, features, and costs. Ordinary lights cannot be used, as the light must be waterproof and pressure proof. Underwater lights exclude water by using an O-ring seal, which should be periodically inspected for wear. Batteries should be stored separately from the light to protect the light from damage by battery leakage.

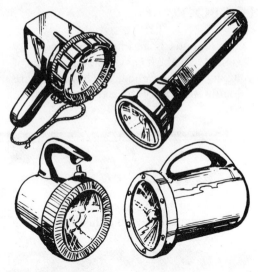

Underwater lights

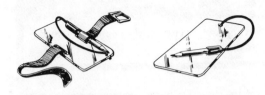

The underwater slate - a useful accessory

UNDERWATER SLATE

This accessory was previously discussed in the section on Communications, because it is very useful for communicating with another diver below the surface. It is also useful for recording times, depths, temperatures, camera settings, or other data. Underwater slates are usually made of plastic and have a pencil attached with a short cord to prevent loss.

SPARE PARTS KIT

This is actually a collection of various accessories kept on hand to save the day when minor equipment problems arise. The items can be stored in a small plastic or rust proof container and carried in your gear bag. Some items to include are:

1. Mask strap
2. Fin strap
3. O-rings
4. Batteries, bulbs
5. Lubricant
6. CO_2 cartridges
7. Snorkel keeper
8. Regulator high pressure plug
9. Small line or twine
10. Neoprene cement (for suit repairs)
11. Waterproof plastic tape
12. Quick release buckle
13. Bailing wire
14. Waterproof matches
15. Pocket knife
16. Pliers
17. Adjustable wrench
18. Screwdriver

A spare parts kit can save the day!

LOGBOOK

The logbook is an important accessory designed to make it easy to keep records of your diving experience. Such records are valuable for proof of experience, dive planning, a record of photos taken or items collected, and to aid in recalling fond memories. Evidence of diving experience with a log is desirable and frequently required. For documentation and more enjoyment, keep a log of all your dives.

Health for Diving

Diving can be strenuous at times, and requires a certain degree of health, fitness, and conditioning to assure safe participation. Enjoyment is increased with confidence which comes from a feeling of well being and readiness.

GOALS

By the end of this module, you should be able to list several health practices favorable for diving, and several which should be avoided by divers.

Follow general health recommendations regarding rest and diet. Do not consume alcoholic beverages before diving. Avoid harmful habits, such as the use of drugs. Diving under the influence of drugs, even some non-prescription drugs, is extremely hazardous. Smoking is a general health hazard, but is a particularly bad habit for divers.

Avoid diving when feeling ill or generally weak, and do not dive with a cold. The use of medications to combat ailments in order to dive is strongly discouraged. One should be in good general health in order to dive.

A person should have a physical examination by a physician familiar with diving when the person first enters the sport, and a subsequent physical examination every two years. Immunizations, particularly tetanus and typhoid, should be kept current.

A good level of physical fitness should be maintained with a regular exercise program. One way to achieve a good level of fitness for diving is to swim with mask, snorkel, and fins at least one half mile three times weekly. Keeping proficient in diving skills

Good health is required for safe diving.

is also necessary. Skills learned in training should be practiced periodically when open water dives cannot be made. After a long period of diving inactivity, divers should first renew their skills in a pool before diving in open water again.

Women have some special health considerations, including menstruation and pregnancy. Unless complications prohibit participation in other sporting activities, diving during menstruation poses no unusual problems. With care and caution, diving may be continued through the early stages of pregnancy, however, experts recommend that the depth be limited to a maximum of 30 feet. Women may also be more susceptible to decompression sickness than men, and should be more conservative with time and depth limits.

You need to be well to dive well. Follow general health recommendations, avoid harmful habits, and keep yourself in shape for diving. This will make your participation easy and pleasurable.

Women have some special considerations for diving but make excellent divers.

Dive Planning

Proper planning helps assure a successful and enjoyable dive. It helps prevent disappointment due to misunderstandings, forgotten items, and poor conditions. Planning your dives is planning your fun! The following steps will guide you in proper dive planning. (Also see Dive Planning Checklist in Appendix)

GOALS

By the end of this module, you should be able to explain the need for dive planning, the steps involved in proper planning of a dive, and several details for each step.

ADVANCE PLANNING

Initial steps involve selecting a buddy and a dive objective. You should pursue similar interests as a team in order to stay together and to have maximum enjoyment through team accomplishment. With an objective in mind, such as lobstering or photography, a dive site can be selected. Consult your log book for reference information if you have dived at the site before. An alternate site should also be chosen in case conditions are unfavorable at the primary location. Determine the best time for the dive. Consult the tide tables, if appropriate, and consider other activity in the area on the date selected. Finally, discuss and agree on logistics, such as how to get there, what to take, and emergency contact information.

Dive planning helps assure success and enjoyment.

PREPARATION

Inspect all equipment needed. Be sure your tank is filled. Gather all gear into one area. Use a checklist of equipment to make sure something isn't forgotten. (See Appendix). Seek information about the dive site and the current diving conditions.

LAST MINUTE PREPARATION

Get a current weather report. File a dive plan with someone not going, leaving information on when you expect to return and what to do if you are delayed. Gather last minute items, such as jacket, hat, sunglasses, wallet, lunch, and log book. Pack gear so the first items needed are on top in your gear bag. Make a final check for all needed items.

PRE-DIVE PLANNING

Upon arrival at the dive site, evaluate the conditions from a vantage point and at the water's edge. Decide whether or not conditions are favorable for diving and for your objectives. If not, go to an alternate site or abort the dive. You should have a good, confident feeling about the situation. If conditions are favorable, decide on entry and exit areas and techniques, and a general course to be followed on the dive.

Discuss hand signals and other communications, buddy system techniques, and what to do if separated. Agree on time, depth, and air supply limits for the dive, and what to do if an emergency should arise. Agree on as much as possible before the dive, when communications are easier through conversation.

DIVE THE PLAN

Planning is of little value if the plans are not carried out. Abide by pre-dive decisions and agreements. Be patient. Diving is the most enjoyable when divers can accomplish an objective together, each anticipating the success and the other's actions. A dive plan need not be complicated, but to get the most from diving, plan your dive, then dive your plan!

Dive Tables Introduction

A quantity of nitrogen is taken up by the body during every dive. The amount absorbed depends upon the depth and duration of the dive. If the quantity of nitrogen in the body exceeds a certain critical amount, decompression sickness will result upon surfacing unless the diver follows a complex procedure of delays in ascent, called decompression, to allow gradual elimination of excess nitrogen. All dives are to be made within established time limits. Dives exceeding these limits require decompression and are beyond the scope of sport diving. Dives not long enough to require decompression are called no-decompression dives. Dives to 33 feet or less have no time limits. As the depth increases, however, the allowable dive time for no-decompression dives decreases.

Following a dive, at least 12 hours are required for the nitrogen level in the body to gradually return to normal. Should a

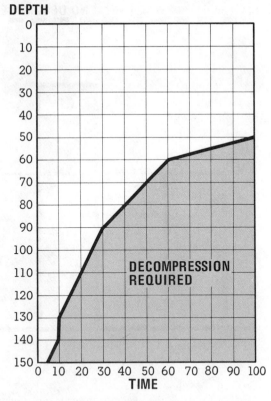

Time/depth limits for avoiding decompression

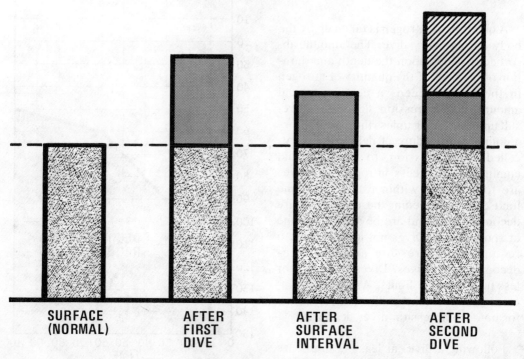

NO DECOMPRESSION LIMIT

SURFACE (NORMAL)   AFTER FIRST DIVE   AFTER SURFACE INTERVAL   AFTER SECOND DIVE

Body nitrogen levels

dive be made within 12 hours of a previous dive, the nitrogen remaining in the system from the previous dive must be taken into consideration. The greater the time between dives, the less nitrogen there will be in the system.

To keep body nitrogen levels within safe limits, tables have been developed by the U.S. Navy (see Appendix) to provide the following information:

1. The maximum time which can be spent at any depth which will allow the diver to ascend directly to the surface without decompression.
2. A classification for the amount of nitrogen remaining in the body after a dive to consider for subsequent dives.
3. The decompression required in the event a diver should accidentally exceed the no-decompression limits.

Do not use the maximum limits provided by the tables. Dive conservatively and well within the no-decompression limits.

GOALS

By the end of this module, you need to be able to explain common dive table terms; use the dive tables to plan No-decompression repetitive dives; to explain the procedures to be used should the No-decompression limits be exceeded; and explain the procedures for flying after diving.

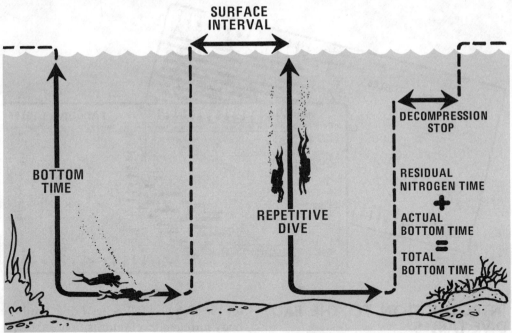

Decompression Tables terminology

DEFINITIONS OF TERMS

1. **Actual Bottom Time:** The total time in minutes from the beginning of descent until the beginning of ascent.

2. **Residual Nitrogen:** Nitrogen remaining in the body after a dive. Twelve hours are required to eliminate excess nitrogen.

3. **Group Designation:** A letter of the alphabet used in the dive tables to designate the amount of Residual Nitrogen in a diver's body after a dive.

4. **Repetitive Dive:** A dive made between 10 minutes and 12 hours of a previous dive. Dives made less than 10 minutes apart are considered a single dive.

5. **Residual Nitrogen Time:** An amount of time, in minutes, added to the bottom time of a repetitive dive to represent the residual nitrogen from a previous dive. The amount is obtained from a table by using the group designation letter.

6. **Total Bottom Time:** The sum of the Residual Nitrogen Time and the Actual Bottom Time of a dive, used to determine a group designation after a repetitive dive.

7. **No-Decompression Limits:** The maximum Total Bottom Time which can be spent at a depth without decompression being required.

8. **Adjusted No-Decompression Limits:** The No-Decompression Limit time less the Residual Nitrogen Time for a specific repetitive dive. Used for planning no-decompression dives. Actual Bottom time is not to exceed the Adjusted No-Decompression Limits.

9. **Decompression Stop:** Remaining at a specified depth for a specified period of time during ascent.

10. **Dive Schedule:** The depth and Total Bottom Time of a dive expressed as Depth/Time, e.g., 90/30 = a dive to 90 feet for 30 minutes.

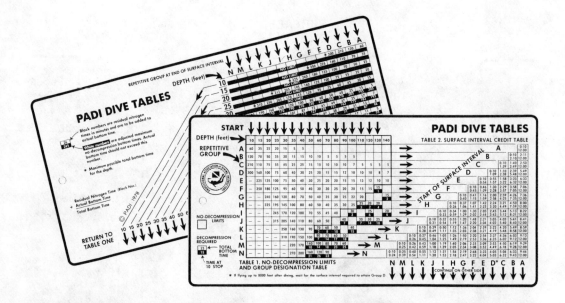

INTRODUCTION TO THE PADI DIVE TABLES

The tables are designed to be used in continuous sequence for no-decompression repetitive diving. There are three tables, each leading to the next.

Table One

Table One is the No-Decompression Limits and Group Designation Table. It provides the maximum limits for Bottom Time, and a letter designation to indicate the amount of nitrogen accumulated from various times at a given depth. The table also indicates delays in ascent necessary in the event the diver mistakenly exceeds the No-Decompression Limits for a depth. This portion of the table is for emergency use only and should not be used for normal diving.

Table Two

Table Two is the Surface Interval Credit Table. It credits the diver for the gradual loss of Nitrogen occurring at the surface

for the 12 hours following a dive until the body nitrogen level returns to normal. Tables Two and Three are only needed when diving repetitively. A diver's Group Designation will change, moving toward the beginning of the alphabet as time goes by, thereby indicating a lower level of nitrogen in the system.

Table Three

Table Three is the Repetitive Dive Timetable, providing two sets of figures, Residual Nitrogen Times and Adjusted No-Decompression Limits for repetitive dives. Residual Nitrogen Time from this table is added to Actual Bottom Time to obtain Total Bottom Time, which is used to obtain another Group Designation from Table One, completing the cycle.

GENERAL RULES

When using the Dive Tables, the following rules need to be observed:

1. Use the exact or next greater number in the tables for the times and depths of all dives. Depths are in feet, and all times are in minutes or hours and

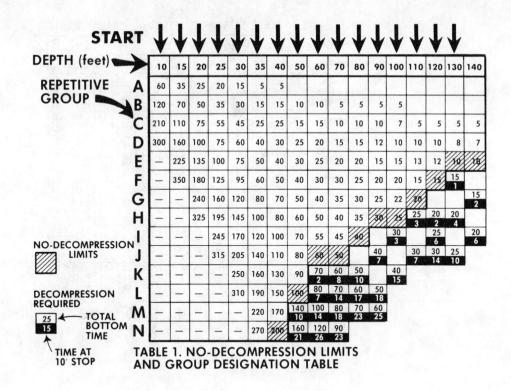

START

DEPTH (feet) →

REPETITIVE GROUP A B C ...

NO-DECOMPRESSION LIMITS

DECOMPRESSION REQUIRED

25 ← TOTAL BOTTOM
15   TIME

TIME AT 10' STOP

TABLE 1. NO-DECOMPRESSION LIMITS AND GROUP DESIGNATION TABLE

Table One

minutes separated by a colon; e.g., 2:10 stands for two hours and 10 minutes.

2. Ascend from all dives at the designated rate of 60 feet per minute. You will learn to estimate the correct rate of ascent during training.
3. Use the schedule for the next deeper depth and next longer time when a dive is cold or strenuous.
4. Plan repetitive dives so each successive dive is to a lesser depth. This aids in nitrogen elimination and decreases the need for decompression.
5. Dives are not to exceed 130 feet in depth, with 100 feet being the recommended limit for sport diving, and 60 feet the recommended limit for novices.

USING THE TABLES

Table One

Enter Table One vertically from the top at the exact or next greater depth reached on a dive. Select the Bottom Time exactly equal to or the next greater number than the Bottom Time of the dive. Follow the column horizontally to the right to obtain the Group Designation for the exposure. For example, a dive to 50 feet for 30 minutes (50/30) would place a diver in Group E. A dive to 52 feet for 27 minutes would place a diver in Group F, since the exact numbers for this dive schedule are not in the tables, the next greater numbers must be used, which would be a schedule of 60/30.

TABLE 2. SURFACE INTERVAL CREDIT TABLE

Start (diagonal)	N	M	L	K	J	I	H	G	F	E	D	C	B	A
A														0:10 12:00
B													0:10 2:10	2:11 12:00
C												0:10 1:39	1:40 2:49	2:50 12:00
D											0:10 1:09	1:10 2:38	2:39 5:48	5:49 12:00
E										0:10 0:54	0:55 1:57	1:58 3:22	3:23 6:32	6:33 12:00
F									0:10 0:45	0:46 1:29	1:30 2:28	2:29 3:57	3:58 7:05	7:06 12:00
G								0:10 0:40	0:41 1:15	1:16 1:59	2:00 2:58	2:59 4:25	4:26 7:35	7:36 12:00
H							0:10 0:36	0:37 1:06	1:07 1:41	1:42 2:23	2:24 3:20	3:21 4:49	4:50 7:59	8:00 12:00
I						0:10 0:33	0:34 0:59	1:00 1:29	1:30 2:02	2:03 2:44	2:45 3:43	3:44 5:12	5:13 8:21	8:22 12:00
J					0:10 0:31	0:32 0:54	0:55 1:19	1:20 1:47	1:48 2:20	2:21 3:04	3:05 4:02	4:03 5:40	5:41 8:40	8:41 12:00
K				0:10 0:28	0:29 0:49	0:50 1:11	1:12 1:35	1:36 2:03	2:04 2:38	2:39 3:21	3:22 4:19	4:20 5:48	5:49 8:58	8:59 12:00
L			0:10 0:26	0:27 0:45	0:46 1:04	1:05 1:25	1:26 1:49	1:50 2:19	2:20 2:53	2:54 3:36	3:37 4:35	4:36 6:02	6:03 9:12	9:13 12:00
M		0:10 0:25	0:26 0:42	0:43 0:59	1:00 1:18	1:19 1:39	1:40 2:05	2:06 2:34	2:35 3:08	3:09 3:52	3:53 4:49	4:50 6:18	6:19 9:28	9:29 12:00
N	0:10 0:24	0:25 0:39	0:40 0:54	0:55 1:11	1:12 1:30	1:31 1:53	1:54 2:18	2:19 2:47	2:48 3:22	3:23 4:04	4:05 5:03	5:04 6:32	6:33 9:43	9:44 12:00

CONTINUE ON OTHER SIDE

Table Two

Table Two

Enter the Surface Interval Credit Table horizontally on the diagonal slope. Move to the right and select the Surface Interval time equal to or between the times shown. Follow the selected column downward to obtain the new Group Designation for the end of the Surface Interval. For example, a dive schedule of 70/20 places a diver in Group E (see Table One). After remaining on the surface for one hour and 30 minutes, the diver wishes to find the new Group Designation. Enter the table along the horizontal line labeled E. A one hour and 30 minute surface interval lies between the times :55 and 1:57. Moving downward in this column, we find the diver's new Group Designation is D. Note the minimum surface interval shown is 10 minutes. If a surface interval is less than 10 minutes, treat the dives as a single dive, adding the bottom times together and using the deepest depth attained on either dive to determine the Group Designation. Short Surface Intervals are discouraged, however.

Table Three

Table Three provides two items of information for repetitive diving. The top figure in each horizontal column is the Residual Nitrogen Time in minutes for a particular Group Designation, and is to be added to the Actual Bottom Time of a dive.

DEPTH (feet)

DEPTH	N	M	L	K	J	I	H	G	F	E	D	C	B	A
10	300	300	300	300	300	300	300	300	300	300	300	210	120	60
							NO LIMIT							
15	350	350	350	350	350	350	350	350	350	225	160	110	70	35
							NO LIMIT							
20	325	325	325	325	325	325	325	240	180	135	100	70	50	25
							NO LIMIT							
25	315	315	315	315	315	245	195	160	125	100	75	55	35	20
							NO LIMIT							
30	310	310	310	250	205	170	145	120	95	75	60	45	30	15
							NO LIMIT							
35	270	220	190	160	140	120	100	80	60	50	40	25	15	5
	40	90	120	150	170	190	210	230	250	260	270	285	295	305
40	213	187	161	138	116	101	87	73	61	49	37	25	17	7
		13	39	62	84	99	113	127	139	151	163	175	183	193
50	142	124	111	99	87	76	66	56	47	38	29	21	13	6
					13	24	34	44	53	62	71	79	87	94
60	107	97	88	79	70	61	52	44	36	30	24	17	11	5
							8	16	24	30	36	43	49	55
70	87	80	72	64	57	50	43	37	31	26	20	15	9	4
							7	13	19	24	30	35	41	46
80	73	68	61	54	48	43	38	32	28	23	18	13	8	4
									12	17	22	27	32	36
90	64	58	53	47	43	38	33	29	24	20	16	11	7	3
									6	10	14	19	23	27
100	57	52	48	43	38	34	30	26	22	18	14	10	7	3
										7	11	15	18	22
110	51	47	42	38	34	31	27	24	20	16	13	10	6	3
											7	10	14	17
120	46	43	39	35	32	28	25	21	18	15	12	9	6	3
												6	9	12
130	40	38	35	31	28	25	22	19	16	13	11	8	6	3
														7

50 60 70 80 90 100 110 120

TABLE 3. REPETITIVE DIVE TIMETABLE

Table Three

The sum of Residual Nitrogen Time and Actual Bottom Time is Total Bottom Time, which is used in Table One to determine the Group Designation for a repetitive dive. The bottom figure in each horizontal line is the Adjusted No-Decompression Limit in minutes for that depth and Group Designation combination. Actual Bottom Time is not to exceed this length of time. In a number of instances in the lower left-hand corner of the table, there are no Adjusted No-Decompression Limits indicated. This is because the Residual Nitrogen Time is so great for those circumstances that decompression would be required. In these cases, dive to a shallower depth, or extend the Surface Interval to attain a lower Group Designation and

Residual Nitrogen Time. An example of the use of Table Three is as follows: A diver with a Group F designation at the end of a Surface Interval plans a dive to 60 feet. At the coordinates F and 60 in Table Three we find 36 over 24. This means the Residual Nitrogen Time is 36 minutes and the Adjusted No-Decompression Limit is 24 minutes. The diver must add 36 minutes Residual Nitrogen Time to the Actual Bottom Time to obtain the Total Bottom Time for the dive, and the Actual Bottom Time must not exceed 24 minutes.

Returning to Table One

To complete the cycle in the use of the tables for repetitive diving, the Total Bottom Time figure for the depth of the repetitive dive is used to re-enter Table One and obtain a group designation for that schedule. If, due to some error, the No-Decompression Limits should be exceeded on a dive, the decompression section (black and white squares) of Table One will need to be used. The top figure indicates Total Bottom Time and the bottom figure indicates the number of minutes which must be spent at a depth of 10 feet during the ascent. For example, a diver with a Total Bottom Time of 36 minutes at 90 feet would use the 90/40 schedule, which requires 7 minutes of decompression at a depth of 10 feet. When decompressing, maintain the chest at the 10 foot depth for the time specified. Do not make any additional dives within 24 hours following an emergency decompression situation. Decompression dives require additional air, surface support, and preparation for emergencies. Avoid decompression situations.

SAMPLE DIVE TABLE PROBLEMS

Table One:
1. What is the Group Designation for a dive:
   1A. to 40 feet for 30 minutes?
   1B. to 51 feet for 25 minutes?
   1C. to 65 feet for 28 minutes?
   1D. schedule of 50/30?
   1E. schedule of 47/26?

Table Two:
2. What is the Group Designation for a:
   2A. Group G diver after a Surface Interval of 1:00? 2:00? 7:35?
   2B. Group F diver after a Surface Interval of :10? 1:40? 2:28?
   2C. Group I diver after a Surface Interval of :34? 4:00? 12:00? 12:01?

Table Three:
3A. What is the maximum No-Decompres-

sion Limit for a Group E diver making a dive to 50 feet?
   3B. What is the Residual Nitrogen Time for this dive?
   3C. What is the Total Bottom Time for the dive if the Actual Bottom Time is 20 minutes?

Table One:
4A. What is the Group Designation for the diver following the dive in the previous question?
   4B. What is the Group Designation for a 40 minute dive to 30 feet by a Group D diver?
   4C. What steps must be taken when surfacing from a dive to 75 feet for 50 minutes?

All Tables:
A dive to 70 feet for 25 minutes is followed by a one hour Surface Interval and another dive to 70 feet.
   5A. What is the Group Designation after the first dive?
   5B. What is the Group Designation after the Surface Interval?
   5C. What is the maximum allowable Bottom Time for the second dive?
   5D. What is the Residual Nitrogen Time for the second dive?
   5E. If the Actual Bottom Time for the second dive is 20 minutes, what will the diver's Group Designation be upon surfacing from the dive?

Answers: 1A = D, 1B = E, 1C = F, 1D = E, 1E = E
2A = F, D, B; 2B = F, D, D; 2C = H, C, A, None
3A = 62 minutes, 3B = 38 minutes, 3C = 58 minutes
4A = H, 4B = G, 4C = Decompress for 10 minutes at 10 feet
5A = F, 5B = E, 5C = 24, 5D = 26, 5E = J

PADI DIVE TABLES

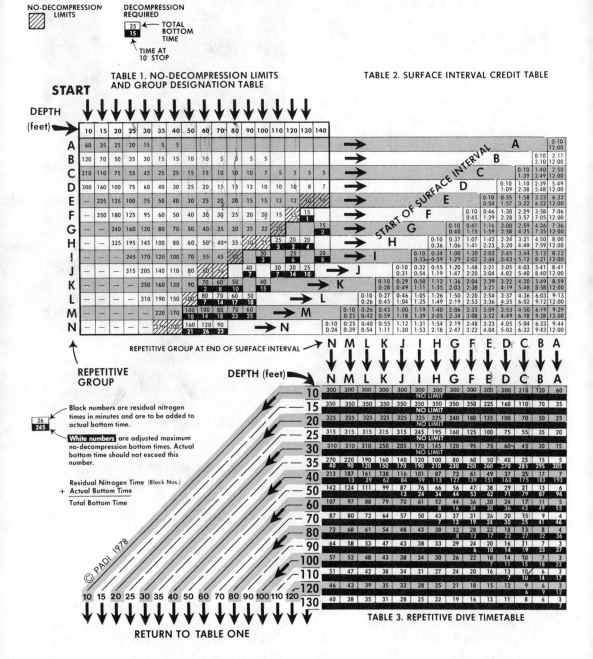

The PADI Dive Tables

PLANNING REPETITIVE DIVES

The intent of the PADI Dive Tables is to make all dives No-Decompression dives. For repetitive diving, proper planning assures dives will be made within the No-Decompression Limits. This can be controlled by limiting the length of the dive, the depth of the dive, and planning Surface Interval duration. Equipment required includes a depth gauge, a slate and pencil, dive tables, and a means to keep track of the amount of time spent underwater. You need to plan no-decompression dives by using the tables and limiting factors to determine no-decompression dive schedules. For a repetitive dive, you need to know the depth of the dive planned, or must limit yourself to a maximum depth for the dive. You also need to know approximately how long you are capable of remaining at the depth. This can be estimated with experience.

Let's plan a repetitive dive to 60 feet as a Group E diver. Referring to Table Three, we find an Adjusted No-Decompression Limit of 30 minutes. This means our Actual Bottom Time must not exceed 30 minutes. This dive could be made within the No-Decompression Limits, so you would be safe to proceed, but what if the diver were in Group G instead? The Actual Bottom Time at 60 feet must not exceed 16 minutes and we are capable of staying for about 25 minutes. We must limit the Actual Bottom Time to less than 16 minutes, dive shallower, or increase the Surface Interval in order to make this dive safely. Suppose, in this situation, we wanted to stay at 60 feet for 25 minutes. How can this be accomplished without exceeding the No-Decompression Limits? All that's needed is to find an Adjusted No-Decompression Limit at 60 feet greater than the 25 minutes we wish to sped there, find the Group Designation yielding that No-Decompression

Limit, and then determine the minimum Surface Interval required to attain that Group Designation. In this instance, the first Adjusted No-Decompression Limit exceeding 25 minutes at 60 feet is 30 minutes, found under the E column. All that is needed is to determine the minimum surface interval for a Group G diver to attain a Group E designation. Refer to Table Two, at the coordinates of G horizontally and E vertically. The minimum time to attain Group E is 1:16, so to make a 25 minute dive to 60 feet without decompression, a Group G diver would need to wait at the surface for at least 1:16 minutes prior to the dive.

Another alternative for the Group G diver is to dive shallower than 60 feet. By diving at 50 feet, the diver could remain 44 minutes, well in excess of the air supply duration. So, diving shallower is a simple solution to situations where Actual Bottom Time is very limited due to residual nitrogen.

The tables should be consulted prior to every repetitive dive to determine the No-Decompression Limits for the dive. Divers should note this on a slate, and also note the No-Decompression Limits for the next greater depths in the event the planned depth is exceeded.

Acquire a Group D designation before flying after diving.

FLYING AFTER DIVING

Following No-Decompression dives, divers may fly safely to a maximum cabin altitude of 8,000 feet if they will first wait the minimum required surface Interval to place them into Group D. For example, a Group H diver should wait at least 2:24 prior to flying.

Divers should wait at least 24 hours before flying after any dives requiring decompression.

Diving Emergencies

Diving is a relatively rugged sport, and the activities often take place in remote areas or far from assistance. While diving is a safe sport in terms of the number of accidents compared to the number of exposures, people do occasionally violate safe diving practices and have a need for assistance, so you may be required to deal with an emergency situation while diving. Should an emergency arise, you need to be able to care for yourself and/or to lend assistance to another diver. To do this, training is required. All divers should be trained in First Aid and Cardio-Pulmonary Resuscitation (CPR), and courses on these topics are presented widely by the American National Red Cross and the American Heart Association. Unless you have recently completed these courses, consult

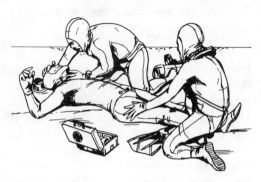

Be trained and prepared for emergencies.

your phone book and enroll for training at your earliest opportunity. The training will be of value to you in ordinary life as well as for any emergency in diving.

Prevention of accidents is preferred, but should an accident occur, you should be able to recognize the situation and provide assistance.

GOALS

By the end of this module, you should be able to:

1. Explain the need for First Aid and CPR training for divers.
2. Describe signs which indicate diver distress.
3. Describe the action to be taken for various diving emergency situations, including cramps, exhaustion, entanglement, and loss of air supply occurring to yourself or to another diver.
4. Explain the general emergency procedures for an unconscious diver.

SELF RESCUE AT THE SURFACE

Most diving distress situations occur at the surface, strange as it may seem. These situations can be avoided or controlled by following some very simple rules: (1) take it easy, and (2) establish buoyancy. Typical problems include exhaustion from swimming against a current or carrying a heavy load; cramping of leg muscles from overexertion or cold; and choking on inhaled water. Each of these situations can be handled with little difficulty by remaining calm and applying simple techniques.

You should not overexert yourself so you get out of breath when diving. If this happens, force yourself to stop, breathe deeply, and recover. If at the surface, buoyancy should be established. Inflate your BCD or discard your weight belt. If you think a problem may be developing, remove your weight belt and hold it close to you. In case the difficulty becomes serious, you will drop the weights automatically, and if the situation improves, you can replace the belt. Avoid any situation where you need to swim, tread water, or exert yourself in order to remain afloat, because exhaustion will occur quickly. Use buoyancy to prevent exhaustion.

Cramps can be removed by stretching the cramped muscle. For cramps in the calf of the leg, pulling up on the tip of the fin works well. Gently massaging a cramped muscle is also helpful. To help prevent recurrence of a cramp, try using a different kick stroke to proceed after the cramp is relieved.

If choking on inhaled water, you can cough into a snorkel or regulator easily, and should do this instead of removing the mouthpiece. Keep the mask in place also. You can also recover more quickly by swallowing several times. Buoyancy is

A cramp in the lower leg can be relieved by stretching the muscle.

valuable in this situation also, as coughing causes a loss in buoyancy from decreased lung volume.

When a problem does occur at the surface, establish buoyancy and take it easy, and don't hesitate to signal for assistance with your whistle or with arm signals. Being assisted when you have a problem in the water is no different than being assisted when you sprain your ankle on land. Get some help to make it easier on yourself.

PROBLEM RECOGNITION

Divers in control of themselves and the situation look just like regular divers even though they may be experiencing some difficulty. You would only recognize their need for assistance by a signal from them. Divers who cannot control themselves or the situation, however, exhibit other subtle signs which need to be recognized before the situation worsens, because these divers do not signal for assistance. A diver who loses control and panics has allowed sudden, unreasoning fear to replace controlled actions with incorrect, instinctive actions. The panicked diver has a feeling of suffocation. Resulting actions are to struggle to hold the head higher out of the water. The mask and mouthpiece are usually removed, requiring even greater effort by the diver to hold the head high to breathe. Movements are fast and jerky, eyes wide and unseeing, and breathing is rapid and shallow. Divers exhibiting these signs need assistance quickly, as they will continue to struggle until completely exhausted and unable to remain afloat.

ASSISTING ANOTHER DIVER

The rules of self rescue apply when assisting another diver in distress. Provide buoyancy for the diver and get him or her to relax, rest, and recover; then help the person out of the water if necessary. Throwing or extending flotation is ideal, however, if this cannot be done, remove the person's weight belt or inflate the BCD.

After establishing buoyancy, talk to the diver, offering encouragement and persuading him or her to take it easy. Allow time to recover, then assist the diver out of the water by accompanying him or her, or using a tired swimmers carry or a tow.

UNDERWATER EMERGENCIES

Few problems occur underwater, and even these can almost always be avoided through awareness. A typical underwater emergency, which can be easily avoided, is running out of air. Even when this occurs, the situation is not serious if divers will stop momentarily, think of the options available, and select a course of action before reacting.

Several options are available to a diver out of air. The first, and easiest, is for the

This diver has reacted incorrectly to a problem and is in distress.

Provide buoyancy to a diver in distress.

diver to make a normal ascent, because the diver is out of air only at depth. As the pressure is decreased during ascent, some additional air can be obtained from the tank. The next option is to breathe from a backup air source, which you are carrying, or which is provided by another diver. If on another diver, you obviously need to know where the unit is located and how to use it. When no back up air source, such as a small redundant scuba unit or an octopus attachment is available, or when your buddy is distant and the water is 30 to 40 feet or less in depth, perform an Emergency Swimming Ascent. This procedure is quite simple, and involves merely swimming to the surface while allowing air to escape from the lungs to prevent lung expansion injuries. Your instructor will explain the procedures for an Emergency Swimming Ascent. It is not a difficult exercise and has been performed successfully from 100 feet or more. If in deep water, however, or if the surface is not directly accessible, you may need to share air with your buddy using a single regulator while ascending if no other source of air is available. This can be easily done when the divers are familiar with the procedure and remain calm. When a buddy breathing ascent is initiated, it should be continued all the way to the surface, rather than switching to a different option during the ascent. The final out-of-air option is an Emergency Buoyant Ascent, which involves ditching weights and/or inflating the BCD to assist in the ascent. This option should be used when doubtful that the surface can be reached by swimming.

You should quickly recognize the need to discuss and agree with your dive buddy regarding the out-of-air emergency procedures for a dive. You need to be familiar with each other's equipment and should review emergency skills, such as buddy breathing, prior to descending. Other general recommendations include a back up air source for depths over 30 to 40 feet and a decrease in the distance separating buddies as the depth increases. Each diver should look after the other, watching air supply, breathing pattern, and time/depth

An emergency swimming ascent is simple and effective.

limits. With each diver alert for himself and the other diver, problems can be avoided and emergency procedures unnecessary.

Entanglement in items such as fishing line, seaweed, or tree branches is another possible underwater problem, but should not be considered an emergency as long as the diver is not injured and has air. If entangled, stop and think, then work slowly and calmly to free yourself, or have your buddy lend assistance. Don't fight or twist to get free. Usually an entanglement will involve the scuba unit, which can be removed, freed, and replaced. Entanglement is not a serious problem if you will deal with it calmly.

THE UNCONSCIOUS DIVER

Your primary concern is to make certain an unconscious diver is breathing, and to

In-water resuscitation is possible and effective.

render artificial respiration if breathing is absent. If the person is unconscious underwater, remove his or her weights, swim the victim to the surface, and begin resuscitation if needed. If you suspect the person's heart has stopped, CPR will be required; and it will be necessary to remove the victim from the water in this case, as it is not possible to administer Cardio-Pulmonary Resuscitation effectively in the water.

There may be a need for artificial respiration or CPR at some time in your diving experience, just as you might have to splint a broken bone on a hiking trip; and recent training in these skills is required in order to be effective. The fundamentals of resuscitation are presented in the Appendix section, but are only minimally helpful. Training courses to learn first aid and resuscitation are recommended for all divers.

If a diving situation has caused unconsciousness in a diver, the following general procedures should be followed:

1. Make sure the person is breathing.
2. Have the victim constantly observed.
3. Lay the victim on the left side, with the entire body inclined so the feet are about 18 inches higher than the head.
4. Keep the victim still and maintain normal body temperature.
5. Administer oxygen if possible.
6. Seek emergency assistance and transport the victim to the nearest recompression chamber.
7. If unable to accompany victim to treatment location, write down as much background information as possible, and attach it conspicuously to the victim.

To be effective in assisting a diver in distress, training is needed.

EMERGENCY CONTACT INFORMATION

You should have information at the dive site on whom to contact locally for a diving emergency. (See the Emergency Procedures Information sheet in the Appendix). This should include phone numbers or radio frequencies for the most appropriate assistance, including paramedics, diving physicians, and recompression chambers. In some areas, special phone numbers have been designated for diving emergencies. Your Instructor should provide this information to you. Include it, along with dimes for phone calls, in your spare parts kit, which accompanies each dive.

SUMMARY

Diving is quite safe when the safety rules are followed, but people do occasionally violate rules, get into difficulty, and may require assistance. To be effective in assisting a diver in distress, training is needed. Completion of at least First Aid and CPR training are recommended, and these skills should also be practiced in diving situations to develop the necessary modifications of techniques. Diver rescue courses are widely taught, and provide excellent training in special procedures for rescues of divers.

More Scuba Skills

GOALS

Your goal is to be able to perform the following skills properly and easily by the end of the fourth Skill Development Session:
1. Weight adjustment for neutral weighting
2. Mid-water buoyancy control
3. Use of an octopus attachment
4. 50 foot horizontal emergency swimming ascent
5. Proficiency Test

PROPER WEIGHTING

You have learned to adjust the amount of weight used to achieve neutral buoyancy at the surface, and now need to demonstrate your ability to do this. Refer to the techniques outlined on page 23.

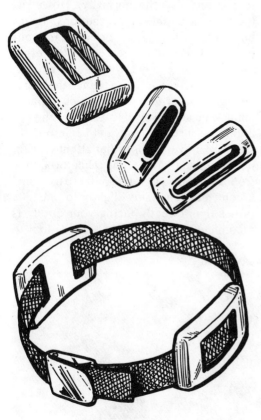

BUOYANCY CONTROL

You have also learned to control your buoyancy by varying the amount of air in your lungs and in your BCD. To demonstrate your control of buoyancy, you need to perform an exercise where you remain suspended in mid-water, completely motionless, maintaining the position with buoyancy control only. To do this, adjust the amount of air in your BCD to achieve neutral buoyancy underwater as explained on page 39, then push yourself

off the bottom and breathe shallowly, using lung volume to maintain a position in mid-water. Breathe shallowly with a neutral lung volume; and if you start to rise, decrease lung volume while continuing to breathe shallowly; and if you start to sink, increase lung volume and continue breathing shallowly. Until familiar with the technique, it is helpful to have a reference nearby, so look at some stationary object and maintain your position in relation to the object.

This exercise has application in diving, as it allows you to stop and hold at any depth during descents and ascents, and makes diving much easier than finning continually to maintain a position.

With control of buoyancy you can hang suspended without support.

OCTOPUS USE

The use of an octopus attachment makes sharing air with a buddy much easier than exchanging a single mouthpiece and is recommended. The technique is quite simple, just put the extra second stage in your mouth and breathe normally. However, there are a couple of precautions. Learn how the unit is to be oriented in your mouth, where it is secured to the other diver, and how to get it when you need it. You should *not* have to signal the other person in order to use the octopus attachment. You should be able to approach your buddy, secure the unit, and begin breathing from it even if his or her attention cannot be gained. Ascending while breathing from an octopus is very similar to a normal ascent, but remaining slightly to one side rather than directly facing your buddy is recommended to allow more freedom to kick.

Use of the octopus attachment greatly simplifies the sharing of air.

Ascending while breathing from an octopus is very similar to a normal ascent.

EMERGENCY SWIMMING ASCENT

An emergency swimming ascent is one of the options available to the diver if the air supply is lost at depth. It is primarily an option to be used when a buddy is not close by to provide air and when the depth is 30 to 40 feet or less. The exercise is quite remarkable in that you start with air in the lungs, exhale all the way to the surface, and upon arrival at the surface still have air in your lungs! This is due, of course, to the expansion of air in the lungs from the decrease in pressure during ascent. The only potential hazard involved is the potential for a lung expansion injury, but this can easily be prevented by **not** holding your breath.

To perform an emergency swimming ascent, simply swim upward with all gear in place, having air escaping constantly during the ascent. Rather than blowing, which is hard to regulate, make a continuous sound "ah" during the ascent. This allows sufficient air to escape from the lungs without resulting in too much air being exhaled. The object is to maintain a lung volume which is neither low nor high, but neutral.

Emergency Swimming Ascent: with all gear in place, make a continuous sound "ah" to maintain neutral lung volume.

Emergency swimming ascents are first practiced while swimming horizontally and making a continuous sound to exhale. You have enough air in your lungs to swim a long way horizontally while exhaling continuously, but 50 feet is sufficient for training. After exhaling continuously for 50 feet while swimming horizontally, it will be very easy to perform an emergency swimming ascent vertically for a shorter distance where air expansion is involved.

Perhaps the greatest value of emergency swimming ascent training is in confidence building. When you realize that there is no cause to panic even if the worst should occur (which is very rare), you will relax, enjoy diving more, and be an improved diver all around.

Practice emergency swimming ascents by swimming horizontally while exhaling. You will be surprised at how far you can travel on a single breath of air.

*Proficiency
testing is
fun and
challenging.*

PROFICIENCY TEST

Now it is time to see how well you have developed the various skills. The following exercises, while not learned specifically, are useful to measure your overall proficiency in addition to the Skill Development Session Tests. You should be able to perform the following with ease;

1. Put your mask on underwater and clear it completely of water with one breath.

2. Wearing mask, snorkel, fins, and a buoyancy control device, swim 200 yards at the surface in less than eight minutes without using your arms.

3. Buddy breathe with another diver, exchanging a single mouthpiece for 50 yards without wearing a mask.

These exercises are not particularly difficult, but are challenging and fun, and allow you to demonstrate your ability to handle yourself and your equipment.

SECTION 5

- **Safety Rules**
- **Diving Opportunities**

Safety Rules

The following summary of Safety Rules for diving will help you to quickly review many of the important points of the course. Refer to this summary periodically to refresh yourself on correct diving practices. These Safety Rules have been separated into four categories: Diving Preparation, Pre-Dive, Diving, and General.

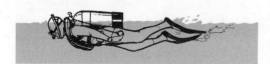

DIVING PREPARATION

1. Have approval for diving from a physician who has given you a thorough medical examination.
2. Be recently trained in First Aid and Cardio-Pulmunary Resuscitation.
3. Keep healthy and fit for diving. Eat right, exercise regularly, and get adequate rest.
4. Keep proficient in diving skills. Practice skills frequently, and review

them before diving after a long period of inactivity in diving.
5. Have **all** equipment needed for local diving conditions.

6. Have scuba equipment serviced annually, and have scuba tanks inspected annually and pressure tested every five years.
7. Maintain your equipment in good condition and inspect it before diving.
8. Fill scuba tanks only with pure, dry, compressed air from reputable air stations.

PRE-DIVE

1. Dive only when feeling well, both physically and mentally. Have a confident feeling about the dive. Be sure the activity is within your capabilities.
2. Know the dive site. Be familiar with the conditions and any hazards.
3. Evaluate the diving conditions and avoid diving when conditions are unfavorable.

4. Get an orientation to any new diving condition or area.
5. Refrain from alcohol or dangerous drugs before diving.
6. Plan the dive with your buddy. Have a common objective. Agree on a general course to follow. Set time and depth limits. Review communications.
7. Plan for no-decompression diving. Consult the dive tables for each dive, allowing a margin of safety. Do not push the limits. Make deepest dives first. Know how to decompress, but avoid the necessity of doing so. Beware of the effects of altitude on diving or on a diver following a dive.
8. Conduct an equipment inspection. Check your own gear and your buddy's gear for misadjustment or malfunction. Know the location and operation of the important parts of your buddy's equipment.

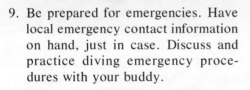

9. Be prepared for emergencies. Have local emergency contact information on hand, just in case. Discuss and practice diving emergency procedures with your buddy.

DIVING

1. Be neutrally weighted for diving. Check your weighting at the surface before diving with new equipment or in water of a different density than normal.
2. Always wear a Buoyancy Control Device for diving. Control buoyancy to make diving easier. Inflate your BCD for surface support.
3. Display the dive flag when diving, and dive nearby.
4. Begin dives against the current, or take current into consideration for the dive. Don't try to swim against a current.
5. Equalize pressure early and often during descent. If pain is felt, ascend until relief is obtained, equalize, and then continue descent.
6. Dive with a buddy and stay together at all times. Know your buddy well and be able to predict reactions. Know the location of your buddy at all times. Agree before the dive on what to do if separated in order to reunite. Decrease separation distance as depth increases.
7. Limit depth to 100 feet or less (60 feet maximum for novices)
8. Treat spear guns as dangerous weapons. Do not have them loaded while out of the water.

9. Avoid contact with unfamiliar life. Move easily and watch what you touch.
10. Dive ahead. Be alert for possible problems and prevent them. Check your equipment and submersible pressure gauge frequently. Have at least 300 psi of air at the end of the dive.
11. Pace yourself. Avoid breathlessness. If winded, stop, rest, and recover before proceeding.
12. Breathe properly. Breathe slowly, deeply, and continuously. Breathe all the time when using scuba, never breath-holding. Exhale slowly and continuously any time the regulator is removed from the mouth. Avoid excessive hyperventilation when skin diving.
13. In an apparent emergency situation, stop, think, and get control, then take action. Act rather than react.
14. Ascend carefully and correctly. Have one hand overhead and look up. Keep breathing. Ascend at 60 feet per minute. Listen for boats.
15. Stop diving when cold or tired. Don't overextend yourself.
16. Dive your plan. Don't revise a dive plan underwater.

GENERAL

1. Be an active diver. Dive at least twelve times annually to keep current.
2. Build experience and capabilities gradually under safe conditions.
3. Keep a log of your diving activities.
4. Continue your diving education. Attend programs, read books and articles, take advanced training, and get training for specialized diving activities.
5. Don't loan your equipment to untrained people, and never attempt to teach another person to dive.

The application of these safety rules will assure safety while allowing complete enjoyment of diving. In short, being prepared, taking it easy, being aware, and using good judgment will prevent any problems in diving.

Diving Opportunities

Upon successful completion of this course you will be certified as a scuba diver, but just what does that mean? Will you be qualified to engage in any activity anywhere? You need to consider what you are qualified to do and then dive within the extent of your qualifications. Although you have learned a great deal thus far in your diving education, there is still much more to be learned. What you need prior to additional knowledge and skills, however, is diving experience. You are not yet truly a diver, but are qualified to become one! You need to apply what you have learned and become quite comfortable and familiar with local open water diving. It is difficult to think of several things at once, but as you repeat experiences, certain actions become automatic and no longer require direct concentration. As this occurs, your mind will be freed to deal with other actions. This is your immediate goal — to gain experience and repeat the required skills of diving until you are comfortable, relaxed, and can perform correctly without having to think through each step. When at this point, you will have more fun while diving, and will be ready to learn other skills to make you an even better diver.

GAINING EXPERIENCE

You have a transition period facing you, to go from a new diver to an experienced diver. This means you need to become familiar with local divers, dive sites, conditions, and diving activities. You need to find experienced divers who can help you do this, and need to know when and where dives are being made. Your Instructor will

provide you with information and references. There may be a local dive club to help introduce you to the real world of sport diving. Various diving societies and associations can be of value. Visit all the local dive stores and dive boats and obtain schedules of their activities. As much as possible, try to dive with a group of experienced divers rather than diving with someone who just completed training with you. Dive with divers who know where to go and how to have fun when they get there. Make your first experiences as great as you can. Get off to a good start. You might even consider a diving vacation to an exotic place where you can increase your experience under ideal conditions and under the direction of a professional dive guide. Numerous dive trips are available at a wide range of prices through some dive stores and many travel agencies.

Dive with experienced divers after your training.

THE NEXT STEP

When you have logged 10 to 15 dives after your initial training, and feel like you would enjoy exploring other diving activities and locations, what should your next step be? Perhaps you feel ready to explore new areas, or to learn Wreck Diving, Underwater Photography, or Search and Recovery diving, but you may not be as prepared as you think. Remember, you can't think of several things at once, and complex activities require your full attention. Diving itself has to be almost automatic for specialty diving — a vehicle to allow you to pursue another activity. Additionally, you do not dive in ideal conditions when engaging in some specialty activities, and need to be able to handle yourself in these new circumstances first, before involvement in an activity. You need to be able to keep track of your position in limited visibility, to find lost objects, to per-

Your first scuba course provides a license to learn to dive. Continue your diving education with advanced and specialty training.

form fine manipulations underwater, and to feel confident of your ability to handle yourself in less than ideal conditions. This is the purpose of the Advanced Open Water Diver Course. You will learn new skills, learn to work underwater, learn to dive in different conditions, and will be introduced to various diving activities. This will allow you to select an interest area which can then be further developed with training from a specialty course on that subject. Round yourself out as a diver by completing advanced training after you have experience and before pursuing a special interest area in diving.

CONTINUING EDUCATION

Diving is constantly improving and changing, and new knowledge is being discovered all the time. You need to keep current with the sport. To do this, you can read diving magazines, newsletters, and books, watch TV programs, attend lectures, conferences, seminars, workshops, and courses, or take tours of various facilities. There are many ways you can keep up with the sport, so take advantage of them, as it will help to make your diving easier and more interesting.

There are numerous books, magazines, and newsletters on diving to add to your knowledge and enjoyment.

WHAT IS THERE TO DO?

Suppose you are an experienced diver, tired of the common, local diving activities. What else is there to do? What can renew your enthusiasm and fan the embers of decreased diving activity into a bright flame of regular, highly enjoyable participation in the sport? The answer lies in new locations, experiences, and activities. Travel to new areas to explore new conditions. Quite often you need not go far, as entirely different conditions frequently exist nearby. Talk to other divers to get ideas. Organize a trip. Strike out on a diving adventure and you will find vast treasures of pleasure underwater in other areas.

Fun comes from success in doing something new, exciting, and challenging. Learning to dive is fun for these reasons. Fun also comes from having new goals and challenges, such as getting good underwater photos, completing a collection of local shells, keeping an aquarium of self collected animals, spearing a large game fish, or finding an ancient wreck. Other people find enjoyment in leadership, journalism, and instruction. The point is that there are many interest areas, probably more than you will ever investigate. More than likely, you will find a hobby to capture your fascination indefinitely, but if you don't, keep looking, for there is a high interest activity in diving for each individual.

SUMMARY

Many opportunities are waiting for you. Just be sure you are trained how to do what you would like to do, and that you use good judgment, not exceeding your capabilities. Diving can be a lifetime adventure for you and your entire family. It is such fun that many change the course of their lives as a result of having learned to dive. The world of diving is an exciting and wonderful place. Welcome to that world. May you use diving opportunities to obtain enjoyment, satisfaction, new friends, and fond memories.

Diving is fun!

APPENDIX

PADI DIVE PLANNING CHECKLIST

Advance Planning:

_____ Dive Buddy(s) _____

_____ Date and time (Check tide tables) _____

_____ Dive Objective _____

_____ Location _____

_____ Alternate Location(s) _____

_____ Directions _____

_____

_____ Meeting place and time _____

_____ Any special or extra gear needed _____

_____ Pre-check of weather and water conditions

Preparation:

_____ Tank(s) filled   _____ Equipment packed

_____ Equipment inspected   _____ Fishing license current

_____ Equipment marked (ID)   _____ Transportation arranged

_____ Spare parts inventoried   _____ Obtain info about new location

_____ Weights adjusted   _____ Get local emergency contact info

Last Minute:

_____ Healthy, rested, nourished

_____ Good, confident feeling about dive

_____ Check weather and water conditions

_____ Final inventory of all needed items

_____ Leave dive plan info with someone not going (Where going, expected time of return, what to do if you do not notify by agreed time)

_____ Pack food, snacks, drinks

_____ Be sure you have: _____Ticket _____Money _____Medications _____Directions _____Swim Suit _____Towel _____Jacket _____Sunglasses Other _____

On-Site:

_____ Evaluate conditions, decide whether or not to dive.

_____ Locate and check nearest communications (telephone, radio)

_____ Select entry/exit points, alternates, methods

_____ Discuss buddy system techniques

_____ Agree on pattern or course for the dive

_____ Agree on limits for the dive (depth, time, minimum air)

_____ Agree on emergency procedures

Problems? Call _____ or _____

PADI OPEN WATER EQUIPMENT CHECKLIST

BASIC EQUIPMENT:

- ☐ Gear Bag
- ☐ Fins, Mask, Snorkel
- Wet Suit:
  - ☐ Jacket
  - ☐ Pants
  - ☐ Vest
  - ☐ Hood
  - ☐ Boots
  - ☐ Gloves
- ☐ Weight Belt
- ☐ Buoyancy Compensator
- ☐ Tank (Filled)
- ☐ Backpack
- ☐ Regulator (with SPG)
- ☐ Compass
- ☐ Depth Gauge

ACCESSORY EQUIPMENT:

- ☐ Float & Flag
- ☐ Knife
- ☐ Watch
- ☐ Thermometer
- ☐ Game Bag
- ☐ Abalone Iron
- ☐ Measuring Device
- ☐ Dive Light
- ☐ Slate and Pencil
- ☐ Marker Buoy
- ☐ Buddy Line
- ☐ Camera, Film
- ☐ Spear
- ☐ Lift Bag

SPARE EQUIPMENT:

- ☐ Tanks
- ☐ Weights
- ☐ Straps
- ☐ O-Rings
- ☐ Tools
- ☐ CO_2 Cartridges
- ☐ Suit Cement
- ☐ Regulator HP Plug
- ☐ Bulbs, Batteries
- ☐ Nylon Line

PERSONAL ITEMS:

- ☐ Swim Suit
- ☐ Towel
- ☐ Jacket
- ☐ Extra Clothes
- ☐ Fishing License
- ☐ Tickets
- ☐ Money
- ☐ Certification Card
- ☐ Log Book
- ☐ Dive Tables
- ☐ Sunglasses
- ☐ Suntan lotion
- ☐ Medications
- ☐ Toilet Articles
- ☐ Lunch, Thermos
- ☐ Cooler Chest
- ☐ Fileting Knife
- ☐ Eating Utensils
- ☐ Sleeping Bag

PADI BOAT DIVING INFORMATION SHEET

Date of trip _____ Name of vessel _____

Landing _____ City _____

Directions _____

Destination _____ Cost _____

Departure time _____ Estimated return time _____

Items needed:

_____ Diving equipment		_____ Suntan lotion
_____ Gear bag		_____ Medication
_____ Extra tank		_____ Ticket
_____ Warm clothes		_____ Money
_____ Jacket		_____ Lunch, snacks
_____ Towel		_____ Drinks

Terminology:

Bow:	Front end of the boat
Stern:	Rear end of the boat
Port:	Left side of the boat when facing bow
Starboard:	Right side of the boat when facing bow
Bridge:	Wheelhouse; vessel control area
Leeward:	The downwind side; sheltered side
Windward:	Side facing into the wind; windy side
Galley:	Kitchen
Head:	Restroom

Instructions:

1. Double check to be sure you have all required equipment and needed items.
2. Board vessel at least one half hour prior to departure time.
3. Ask crew where and how to stow your gear.
4. Place clothes, cameras, lunch and all items to be kept dry inside, and all diving equipment outside on the deck.
5. Wait in the stern area for pre-departure briefing.
6. Keep dockside rail clear during docking operations.
7. If susceptible to seasickness, take medication prior to departure.
8. If seasick, use the leeside rail, not the head.
9. Learn toilet operation and rules before using head.
10. Stay off the bow during anchoring operations.
11. Work out of your gear bag. No loose gear on deck.
12. Check out and check in with the Divemaster for all dives.
13. Pack and stow all gear before return trip.
14. Be available for *visual* roll call before boat is moved.
15. Check to be sure nothing is left behind when disembarking.

Rules:

1. No trash or litter overboard. Use trash cans.
2. Bridge and engine room are off limits.
3. Do not sit on the rails when underway.
4. Follow the instructions of the crew.

DIVER'S FIRST AID KIT

First Aid Book
Two dimes taped to emergency phone number card
Band Aids
Aspirin and/or Midol
Triangle Bandages (3 or more)
Gauze Roller Bandages
Tourniquet
Soap (Antibacterial)
Razor Blades or Exacto Knife
Tweezers or Forceps (fine tipped)
Needles
Safety Pins
Mild Antiseptic (Hydrogen Peroxide, Listerine)
Snake Bite Kit
Waterproof Matches
Water Heating Device (Sterno)

If room is available:
      Scissors
      Side Cutting Pliers
      Adhesive Tape
      Q-Tips
      Tongue Depressors
      Paper Cups
      Salt
      Gauze Scrub Pads
      Chapstick

Also have available:
      Blanket of some type
      Drinking water

Other possibilities:
      Sea Sting Kit Model SSK (Dacor Corp.)

All items can be carried in a small plastic tackle box.

PADI EMERGENCY PROCEDURES
INFORMATION SHEET

Date _____   Exact Location _____

Emergency Phone Numbers:

Fire Department _____   Police _____

Coast Guard _____   Chamber _____

Hospital _____   Other _____

Nearest diving doctor _____   Phone _____

Nearest recompression chamber _____

Chamber address _____

Directions _____

Emergency Radio Frequencies: 2182 KHZ, 156.8 MHZ   Your call letters _____

Sample Emergency Information Card for Divers
(Can be used as original for printing)

(Front)

DIVER EMERGENCY INFORMATION CARD

Name _____ Birth Date _____

Address _____

In emergency contact _____

Address _____ Phone ( ) _____

Medical Alert Info _____

Required Medications _____ Blood Type _____

Personal Physician _____ Phone ( ) _____

In an emergency, I hereby authorize medical treatment and/or treatment in a recompression chamber.

_____   _____
Signature   Date

Signature of parent or guardian if under age 18

(Back)

INFORMATION TO BE SENT WITH VICTIM IN AN EMERGENCY:

Background of accident _____

Symptoms observed _____

_____ Time _____

First Aid Given _____

_____ Time _____

CARDIOPULMONARY RESUSCITATION (CPR)

		AIRWAY CLOSED	AIRWAY OPENED
IF UNCONSCIOUS **A** AIRWAY OPENED	- Lift Neck - Extend Head		

IF NOT
BREATHING
 	
B
 	
BREATHING
RESTORED
	- Pinch Nose
	- Open Your Mouth
	- Seal Around Lips
	- Inflate Lungs - -
	   Watch Chest Rise
	- Remove Your Mouth
	- Repeat 12 Times /Min
	  - 20 - 30 Times/Min
	     for Children

IF PULSELESS	- Compress Lower Half but not tip of Sternum - 60 - 80 Compressions/Min	
C CIRCULATION RESTORED	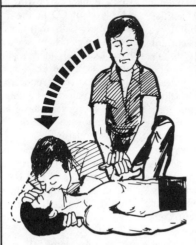 ONE RESCUER - 15 Chest Compressions - 2 Quick Lung Inflations	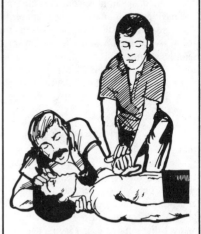 TWO RESCUERS - 5 Chest Compressions - 1 Interposed Lung Inflation

PADI

PURE AIR PROGRAM

Air from most scuba tanks would make Mother Nature ashamed of her Rocky Mountain breezes. Before the air is good enough for the diver to use, it has been filtered, heated, dried, and chemically treated until it is pure and safe for use underwater.

Compressors pumping air for human use are severely regulated by a myriad of laws, all of which specify that what goes into a tank must exceed in quality the freshest air in nature. Yet it is possible to get a tank of bad air, whether it be a toxic contaminant or just a plain unpleasant odor. The quality of air supplied and the condition and configuration of the equipment varies greatly from store to store, and boat to boat. While fatalities occurring from contaminated air have been few, there have been many cases of nausea or other illness caused by impure, compressed air.

To assure divers they are getting the best compressed air available, the Professional Association of Diving Instructors conducts a Pure Air Program. The program is essentially one of taking compressed air samples from participating facilities and having the air analyzed by a reliable laboratory. Air samples must meet or exceed the current strictest accepted standards for divers. If the air samples do not meet the standards, then the operator of the compressed air plant must do whatever is necessary to achieve air of suitable quality.

To improve air quality, the operator must have a knowledge of the causes of impure air and its affect on divers, and the steps necessary to obtain pure air. The first consideration in a system that will deliver pure air is to establish a definition of pure air for underwater use. We know that air is a mixture of gases, roughly 78 percent nitrogen, 21 percent oxygen, and one percent other atmospheric trace gases. Atmospheric air also contains water vapor, dust, soot, hydrocarbons, and many other impurities in varying degrees. In special situations any one of these may be present in very high concentrations. Air is graded by limiting the concentration of specific trace constituents as shown by the following table.

	U.S. NAVY*	Compressed Gas Assoc.**
Oxygen	20 - 22%	19 - 23%
Maximum Carbon Dioxide	0.05% (500 ppm)	0.10% (1000 ppm)
Maximum Carbon Monoxide	0.002% (20 ppm)	0.002% (20 ppm)
Maximum Oil Vapor	5 mg/m^3	5 mg/m^3
Particles Solid & Liquid	None detectable	
Odor	Not Objectionable	

*U.S. Navy Diving Manual, p. 5-18 (1973), NAVSHIPS 0994-001-9010
**Compressed Gas Association Pamphlet, G7.1

In urban areas carbon monoxide (CO) may be present in free air at rather high levels, in some cases as high as 50-100 parts per million (ppm). The level of CO in the atmosphere varies from a low of 25 ppb to values as high as 81 ppm in Los Angeles. There are 17 cities in America that have CO levels in excess of 10 ppm 50% of the time over a one year average. The atmosphere is thus a source of concern to diving as this contaminated air may be compressed and supplied to divers. Moreover, the level of CO in air that may be compressed for air diving may exceed proposed standards.

Also, Carbon monoxide occurs in high concentration in cigarette smoke and the average concentration inhaled is 400 to 500 ppm. A smoking diver already has his blood polluted with a level that exceeds what he would acquire if he were exposed to air containing 20 ppm CO for 12 hours.

Other impurities such as dust and oxides of sulfur are also present in the atmosphere. These contaminants come from such sources as industrial and automotive exhausts. In addition to the contaminants that may be present in free air, air compressor machinery may also add contaminants. These include oil vapor, hydrocarbons from the compressor motor exhausts, and oil breakdown products from the compressor lubricant. All of these must be avoided or removed before compressed air is suitable for diver use.

The location of the compressor intake with respect to possible sources of contamination is fully as important as any single factor in assuring satisfactory air quality. Compressors should not be operated near the exhausts of internal combustion engines, sewer manholes, sandblasting, painting, electric arcs, or sources of smoke. Intakes must be provided with filters for removing dust and other particles in the respirable size range. Proper orientation to wind direction is also a critical factor in setting up air compressor systems.

FILTERING SYSTEMS

Air leaving a compressor must be cleaned and filtered prior to storage or immediate use. In some compressor systems the compressed gas is passed through an oil and moisture separator to remove entrained oil, mist, and excessive moisture. This is followed by passage through a filter system to remove excess water, oil particulate matter, and odor.

Recently developed systems are on the market that more effectively remove contaminants (National Safety Council 1973). They are designed to remove carbon monoxide, oil vapor, nitrogen dioxide, odor, and taste contaminants. One such system does this by the oxidation of carbon monoxide to carbon dioxide through chemisorption and catalysis with a material called Hopcalite. Hopcalite is a true catalyst in this reaction and is neither consumed nor exhausted in the process until it is deactivated by water vapor. The amount of carbon dioxide produced by the catalytic action is insignificant.

The amount of oxygen used up is approximately 0.5 part per million of carbon monoxide and has no appreciable effect on the air produced. Nitrogen dioxide is also removed from the air by a combination of adsorption and chemical reaction. Activated carbon is used to absorb odor and taste.

PADI PURE AIR ANALYSIS PROGRAM

PADI provides an air analysis service through a national testing laboratory and strongly recommends all air stations use these facilities. Stores who are presently having their air analyzed locally may participate in this program provided they abide by the standards and pay an annual service charge for filing and handling.

A "Pure Air Station" certificate is issued to stores that participate in the Pure Air Program. The store takes air samples regularly from each compressor and has the air analyzed. Results of the analysis is reported to PADI Headquarters. If the analysis is approved, a gold seal will be issued for that particular analysis to be affixed to the certificate.

Equipment for obtaining meaningful air samples from compressed air supplies has been developed and is in current use on a number of sampling programs. The system employs a method that lowers the pressure of air supplies to less than three atmospheres absolute pressure, which, in turn, reduces the size and weight of the equipment and containers needed to obtain the samples. The equipment is safe and readily transportable by any mode of transportation including U.S. priority mail and United Parcel Service.

Through the PADI Pure Air Program, the diving industry has been provided with its first and only ongoing program of regular air analysis. The analysis is provided by the Texas Research Institute, the leading company in the United States for air analysis. The responsible retailers of the PADI Training Facility program have voluntarily joined together to participate in the Pure Air program and have set aside a portion of their profits to pay for this service. PADI urges you to support the dealer who displays the Pure Air Station emblem.

U.S. NAVY AIR DECOMPRESSION TABLE

NO-DECOMPRESSION LIMITS AND REPETITIVE GROUP DESIGNATION TABLE FOR NO-DECOMPRESSION AIR DIVES

Depth (feet)	No-decompression limits (min)	A	B	C	D	E	F	G	H	I	J	K	L	M	N	O
10		60	120	210	300											
15		35	70	110	160	225	350									
20		25	50	75	100	135	180	240	325							
25		20	35	55	75	100	125	160	195	245	315					
30		15	30	45	60	75	95	120	145	170	205	250	310			
35	310	5	15	25	40	50	60	80	100	120	140	160	190	220	270	310
40	200	5	15	25	30	40	50	70	80	100	110	130	150	170	200	
50	100		10	15	25	30	40	50	60	70	80	90	100			
60	60		10	15	20	25	30	40	50	55	60					
70	50			5	10	15	20	30	35	40	45	50				
80	40			5	10	15	20	25	30	35	40					
90	30			5	10	12	15	20	25	30						
100	25			5	7	10	15	20	22	25						
110	20				5	10	13	15	20							
120	15				5	10	12	15								
130	10				5	8	10									
140	10				5	7	10									
150	5				5											
160	5					5										
170	5					5										
180	5					5										
190	5					5										

Group Designation

Repetitive group at the beginning of the surface interval

Surface interval time table (each group: start time / end time of interval):

Group	Intervals (start – end)
A	0:10–12:00*
B	0:10–2:10 / 2:11–12:00*
C	0:10–1:39 / 1:40–2:49 / 2:50–12:00*
D	0:10–1:09 / 1:10–2:38 / 2:39–5:48 / 5:49–12:00*
E	0:10–0:54 / 0:55–1:57 / 1:58–3:22 / 3:23–6:32 / 6:33–12:00*
F	0:10–0:45 / 0:46–1:29 / 1:30–2:28 / 2:29–3:57 / 3:58–7:05 / 7:06–12:00*
G	0:10–0:40 / 0:41–1:15 / 1:16–1:59 / 2:00–2:58 / 2:59–4:25 / 4:26–7:35 / 7:36–12:00*
H	0:10–0:36 / 0:37–1:06 / 1:07–1:41 / 1:42–2:23 / 2:24–3:20 / 3:21–4:49 / 4:50–7:59 / 8:00–12:00*
I	0:10–0:33 / 0:34–0:59 / 1:00–1:29 / 1:30–2:02 / 2:03–2:44 / 2:45–3:43 / 3:44–5:12 / 5:13–8:21 / 8:22–12:00*
J	0:10–0:31 / 0:32–0:54 / 0:55–1:19 / 1:20–1:47 / 1:48–2:20 / 2:21–3:04 / 3:05–4:02 / 4:03–5:40 / 5:41–8:40 / 8:41–12:00*
K	0:10–0:28 / 0:29–0:49 / 0:50–1:11 / 1:12–1:35 / 1:36–2:03 / 2:04–2:38 / 2:39–3:21 / 3:22–4:19 / 4:20–5:48 / 5:49–8:58 / 8:59–12:00*
L	0:10–0:26 / 0:27–0:45 / 0:46–1:04 / 1:05–1:25 / 1:26–1:49 / 1:50–2:19 / 2:20–2:53 / 2:54–3:36 / 3:37–4:35 / 4:36–6:02 / 6:03–9:12 / 9:13–12:00*
M	0:10–0:25 / 0:26–0:42 / 0:43–0:59 / 1:00–1:18 / 1:19–1:39 / 1:40–2:05 / 2:06–2:34 / 2:35–3:08 / 3:09–3:52 / 3:53–4:49 / 4:50–6:18 / 6:19–9:28 / 9:29–12:00*
N	0:10–0:24 / 0:25–0:39 / 0:40–0:54 / 0:55–1:11 / 1:12–1:30 / 1:31–1:53 / 1:54–2:18 / 2:19–2:47 / 2:48–3:22 / 3:23–4:04 / 4:05–5:03 / 5:04–6:32 / 6:33–9:43 / 9:44–12:00*
O	0:10–0:23 / 0:24–0:36 / 0:37–0:51 / 0:52–1:07 / 1:08–1:24 / 1:25–1:43 / 1:44–2:04 / 2:05–2:29 / 2:30–2:59 / 3:00–3:33 / 3:34–4:17 / 4:18–5:16 / 5:17–6:44 / 6:45–9:54 / 9:55–12:00*
Z	0:10–0:22 / 0:23–0:34 / 0:35–0:48 / 0:49–1:02 / 1:03–1:18 / 1:19–1:36 / 1:37–1:55 / 1:56–2:17 / 2:18–2:42 / 2:43–3:10 / 3:11–3:45 / 3:46–4:29 / 4:30–5:27 / 5:28–6:56 / 6:57–10:05 / 10:06–12:00*

RESIDUAL NITROGEN TIMES (MINUTES)

REPETITIVE DIVE DEPTH	Z	O	N	M	L	K	J	I	H	G	F	E	D	C	B	A
40	257	241	213	187	161	138	116	101	87	73	61	49	37	25	17	7
50	169	160	142	124	111	99	87	76	66	56	47	38	29	21	13	6
60	122	117	107	97	88	79	70	61	52	44	36	30	24	17	11	5
70	100	96	87	80	72	64	57	50	43	37	31	26	20	15	9	4
80	84	80	73	68	61	54	48	43	38	32	28	23	18	13	8	4
90	73	70	64	58	53	47	43	38	33	29	24	20	16	11	7	3
100	64	62	57	52	48	43	38	34	30	26	22	18	14	10	7	3
110	57	55	51	47	42	38	34	31	27	24	20	16	13	10	6	3
120	52	50	46	43	39	35	32	28	25	21	18	15	12	9	6	3
130	46	44	40	38	35	31	28	25	22	19	16	13	11	8	6	3
140	42	40	38	35	32	29	26	23	20	18	15	12	10	7	5	2
150	40	38	35	32	30	27	24	22	19	17	14	12	9	7	5	2
160	37	36	33	31	28	26	23	20	18	16	13	11	9	6	4	2
170	35	34	31	29	26	24	22	19	17	15	13	10	8	6	4	2
180	32	31	29	27	25	22	20	18	16	14	12	10	8	6	4	2
190	31	30	28	26	24	21	19	17	15	13	11	10	8	6	4	2

U.S. NAVY AIR DECOMPRESSION TABLE

Depth (feet)	Bottom time (min)	Time first stop (min:sec)	Decompression stops (feet)					Total ascent (min:sec)	Repetitive group
			50	40	30	20	10		
40	200						0	0:40	*
	210	0:30					2	2:40	N
	230	0:30					7	7:40	N
	250	0:30					11	11:40	O
	270	0:30					15	15:40	O
	300	0:30					19	19:40	Z
50	100						0	0:50	*
	110	0:40					3	3:50	L
	120	0:40					5	5:50	M
	140	0:40					10	10:50	M
	160	0:40					21	21:50	N
	180	0:40					29	29:50	O
	200	0:40					35	35:50	O
	220	0:40					40	40:50	Z
	240	0:40					47	47:50	Z
60	60						0	1:00	*
	70	0:50					2	3:00	K
	80	0:50					7	8:00	L
	100	0:50					14	15:00	M
	120	0:50					26	27:00	N
	140	0:50					39	40:00	O
	160	0:50					48	49:00	Z
	180	0:50					56	57:00	Z
	200	0:40				1	69	71:00	Z
70	50						0	1:10	*
	60	1:00					8	9:10	K
	70	1:00					14	15:10	L
	80	1:00					18	19:10	M
	90	1:00					23	24:10	N
	100	1:00					33	34:10	N
	110	0:50				2	41	44:10	O
	120	0:50				4	47	52:10	O
	130	0:50				6	52	59:10	O
	140	0:50				8	56	65:10	Z
	150	0:50				9	61	71:10	Z
	160	0:50				13	72	86:10	Z
	170	0:50				19	79	99:10	Z
80	40						0	1:20	*
	50	1:10					10	11:20	K
	60	1:10					17	18:20	L
	70	1:10					23	24:20	M
	80	1:00				2	31	34:20	N
	90	1:00				7	39	47:20	N
	100	1:00				11	46	58:20	O
	110	1:00				13	53	67:20	O
	120	1:00				17	56	74:20	Z
	130	1:00				19	63	83:20	Z
	140	1:00				26	69	96:20	Z
	150	1:00				32	77	110:20	Z
90	30						0	1:30	*
	40	1:20					7	8:30	J
	50	1:20					18	19:30	L
	60	1:20					25	26:30	M
	70	1:10				7	30	38:30	N
	80	1:10				13	40	54:30	N
	90	1:10				18	48	67:30	O
	100	1:10				21	54	76:30	Z
	110	1:10				24	61	86:30	Z
	120	1:10				32	68	101:30	Z
	130	1:00			5	36	74	116:30	Z

* See No Decompression Table for repetitive groups

U.S. NAVY AIR DECOMPRESSION TABLE

Depth (feet)	Bottom time (min)	Time first stop (min:sec)	Decompression stops (feet) 50	40	30	20	10	Total ascent (min:sec)	Repetitive group
100	25						0	1:40	*
	30	1:30					3	4:40	I
	40	1:30					15	16:40	K
	50	1:20				2	24	27:40	L
	60	1:20				9	28	38:40	N
	70	1:20				17	39	57:40	O
	80	1:20				23	48	72:40	O
	90	1:10			3	23	57	84:40	Z
	100	1:10			7	23	66	97:40	Z
	110	1:10			10	34	72	117:40	Z
	120	1:10			12	41	78	132:40	Z
110	20						0	1:50	*
	25	1:40					3	4:50	H
	30	1:40					7	8:50	J
	40	1:30				2	21	24:50	L
	50	1:30				8	26	35:50	M
	60	1:30				18	36	55:50	N
	70	1:20			1	23	48	73:50	O
	80	1:20			7	23	57	88:50	Z
	90	1:20			12	30	64	107:50	Z
	100	1:20			15	37	72	125:50	Z
120	15						0	2:00	*
	20	1:50					2	4:00	H
	25	1:50					6	8:00	I
	30	1:50					14	16:00	J
	40	1:40				5	25	32:00	L
	50	1:40				15	31	48:00	N
	60	1:30			2	22	45	71:00	O
	70	1:30			9	23	55	89:00	O
	80	1:30			15	27	63	107:00	Z
	90	1:30			19	37	74	132:00	Z
	100	1:30			23	45	80	150:00	Z
130	10						0	2:10	*
	15	2:00					1	3:10	F
	20	2:00					4	6:10	H
	25	2:00					10	12:10	J
	30	1:50				3	18	23:10	M
	40	1:50				10	25	37:10	N
	50	1:40			3	21	37	63:10	O
	60	1:40			9	23	52	86:10	Z
	70	1:40			16	24	61	103:10	Z
	80	1:30		3	19	35	72	131:10	Z
	90	1:30		8	19	45	80	154:10	Z
140	10						0	2:20	*
	15	2:10					2	4:20	G
	20	2:10					6	8:20	I
	25	2:00				2	14	18:20	J
	30	2:00				5	21	28:20	K
	40	1:50			2	16	26	46:20	N
	50	1:50			6	24	44	76:20	O
	60	1:50			16	23	56	97:20	Z
	70	1:40		4	19	32	68	125:20	Z
	80	1:40		10	23	41	79	155:20	Z

* See No Decompression Table for repetitive groups

ENGLISH-METRIC CONVERSIONS

At some time or other, divers will find themselves struggling to convert cubic feet into cubic centimetres or something equally as irritating. The following figures will help you:

Length

1 inch	=	2.540 centimetres
1 foot	=	0.304 metres
1 yard	=	0.914 metres
1 fathom	=	1.828 metres or 6.0 feet
1 statute mile (5280 feet)	=	1.609 kilometres
1 nautical mile (6080 feet)	=	1.853 kilometres
1 centimetre	=	0.393 inches
1 metre	=	3.280 feet
1 metre	=	1.093 yards
1 metre	=	0.546 fathoms
1 kilometre	=	0.621 statute miles
1 kilometre	=	0.539 nautical miles

Capacity

1 cubic inch	=	16.378 cubic centimetres
1 cubic foot	=	0.028 cubic metres
1 cubic foot	=	28.317 litres
1 cubic yard	=	0.764 cubic metres
1 pint	=	0.568 litres
1 gallon	=	4.546 litres
1 cubic centimetre	=	0.061 cubic feet
1 cubic metre	=	35.314 cubic feet
1 cubic metre	=	1.308 cubic yards
1 litre (1,000 c.c.)	=	0.035 cubic feet
1 litre	=	0.220 gallons
1 litre	=	1.760 pints

Weight

1 ounce	=	28.349 grams
1 pound	=	0.454 kilograms
1 long ton	=	1.016 metric tons
1 long ton	=	1.016 kilograms
1 kilogram	=	2.205 pounds
1 metric ton	=	0.984 long tons
1 metric ton	=	2,205 pounds

PRESSURE

1 pound per square inch	=0.073 kilograms per square centimetre
1 kilogram per square centimetre	=14.223 pounds per square inch
1 atmosphere	=14.7 pounds per square inch
1 atmosphere	=1.033 kilograms per square centimetre

ENGLISH - METRIC CONVERSIONS (CONTINUED)

WATER

1 cubic foot of fresh water weighs 62.5 pounds approx.
1 cubic foot of average salt water weighs 64 pounds approx.
1 gallon of water weighs 8 pounds approx.

TEMPERATURE

To convert degrees Fahrenheit to degrees Centigrade, deduct 32 and multiply
by 5/9.
To convert degrees Centigrade to degrees Fahrenheit, multiply by 9/5 and
add 32.

CONVERSIONS (APPROXIMATE)

Miles to kilometres......................................	multiply by 8/5
Kilometres to miles.....................................	multiply by 5/8
Statute miles to nautical miles....................	deduct 1/8
Nautical miles to statute miles....................	add 1/7
Pounds per square inch (p.s.i.) to atmospheres......................................	divide by 14.7
Atmospheres or bars to kilos per square centimetre..	nearly the same
Water depth (feet) to bars absolute............	divide by 33 and add 1 bar
Water depth (metres) to bars absolute........	divide by 10 and add 1 bar
Bars absolute to feet of water depth...........	subtract 1 bar and multiply by 33
Bars absolute to metres of water depth.......	subtract 1 bar and multiply by 10

WIND - DIRECTION, SPEED AND MEASUREMENT

Direction	Wind direction is always specified as the direction from which the wind blows. (A Westerly wind blows from West to East.)
Speed	Wind speed is expressed in knots (a knot is a speed of one nautical mile per hour) by mariners and airmen and in miles per hour by landsmen and coastal navigators.

Conversions	1 knot	=1.7 feet per second approx.
		=0.51 metres per second approx.
	1 mile per hour	=1-1/2 feet per second approx.
		=1.609 kilometres per hour approx.
	1 foot per second	=2/3 miles per hour approx.
		=0.3 metres per second approx.
	1 kilometre per hour	=5/8 miles per hour approx.
	1 metre per second	=3-1/3 feet per second approx.

INFORMATION SOURCES

ACDE
(Assn. of Commercial Diving
  Education)
Box 36
Summerland, CA 93067

California Wreck Divers
Box 9922
Marina Del Rey, CA 90291

CBOA
(Charter Boat Owners Assn.)
Bud Wolfe
332 S. Bedford Drive
Beverly Hills, CA 90212

CMAS
(World Underwater Federation)
34 Rue du Colisee
Paris 8, France

CNCA
(Council for National Cooper-
  ation in Aquatics)
220 Ashton Road
Ashton, MD 20702

CURO
(Council of Resort Operators)
Box 530173
Miami, FL 33153

DEMA
(Diving Equipment Manufac-
  turers Association)
Box 3212
Torrance, CA 90503

Dive Canada (Magazine)
559 Jarvis Street
Toronto, Ontario, Canada

Global Mfg. Corporation
(Publications)
Box 15307
Milwaukee, WI 53215

IOF
(International Oceanographic
  Foundation)
3979 Rickenbacker Causeway
Virginia Key
Miami, FL 33149

NACD
(National Assn. of Cave Divers)
2900 N.W. 29th Avenue
Gainsville, FL 32605

NASAR
(National Assn. for Search and
  Recovery)
Box 2123
La Jolla, CA 92038

NOAA
(Sea Grant)
Division of Marine Resources
University of Washington
  HG-30
Seattle, WA 98195

NSTC
(National Scuba Training
  Council)
Box 7666
Long Beach, CA 90807

Pacific Diver (Magazine)
Seagraphic Publications Ltd.
1520 Alberni Street
Vancouver, B.C., Canada

Presidential Sports Award
Box 1412
Annex Station
Providence, R.I. 02904

Skin Diver (Magazine)
8490 Sunset Boulevard
Los Angeles, CA 90069

Sport Diver (Magazine)
103 Century 21 Drive,
  Suite 120
Jacksonville, FL 32216

Undercurrents (Magazine)
Box 1658
Sausalito, CA 94965

UMS
(Undersea Medical Society)
9650 Rockville Pike
Bethesda, MD 20014

University of Rhode Island
National Underwater Accident
  Data Center
Box 68
Kingston, RI 02881

UPS
(Underwater Photographic
  Society)
Box 7088
Van Nuys, CA 91409

USA
(Underwater Society of
  America - Dive Club Informa-
  tion)
238 Sunset
Glen Ellyn, IL 60137

USGPO
(U.S. Government Printing
  Office)
Superintendent of Documents
Washington, D.C. 20402

INDEX

A

Activities, 85-86, 151
Advanced Diving, 148-149
Air, 95, 160-161
   consumption, 51
   density, 48
   expansion, 49-51
   purity, 95, 160-161
   spaces, 49-50
Airway Control, 29, 132
Algae, 80
Altitude, 98
Animals, 83-84
Aquatic Plants, 84
Ascending, 42-43, 75
Assistance, 133
Atmospheric Pressure, 10, 47

B

Backpacks, 56, 77
Basic Scuba Diver, 3-5
Bends; see Decompression Sickness
Blackout, 27
Blast Clearing, 36-37
Boat Diving, 108, 156
Boots, 21
Bottom Composition, 82
Bottom Time, 123
Breathing, 26-29
   resistance, 15, 51, 58
   without a mask, 73-74
   buddy, 104
Buddy System, 66-67
Buoyancy, 8-10
   check, 24, 39
   control, 103, 137
   control device, 18-19, 30, 39,
      102-103
Buoyant Ascent, 134
Burst Disc, 54

C

Cardio-Pulmonary Resuscitation (CPR),
   131, 135, 159
Certification, 3-4
Chamber; see Recompression Chamber
Choking, 29, 132
Cold, 7-8, 80
Collecting Bags, 116
Color Absorption, 7
Communications, 62-65
Compass, 93, 112-113
Console; see Instrument Panel
Contaminated Air, 95-96
Continuing Education, 3, 149
Cramps, 17, 132
Currents, 81-82
Cylinders; see Tanks

D

Decompression, 98, 123
   meter, 98
   sickness, 97
   tables, 162-164
Density, 6, 8, 82
Depth Gauge, 92-93
Descending, 41, 75, 111
Descent Line, 81, 111
Directional Control, 42
Disassembly of Scuba, 77
Disorientation, 81
Displacement Clearing, 37
Dive
   flag, 116
   knife, 24
   planning, 119-120, 154
   tables, 121-131
   watch, 92
DOT (Dept. of Transportation), 53
Drag, 8
Dry Suit; see Exposure Suit

168

E

Ears, 11, 50
Education, 2-3, 149
Emergencies, 131-136, 158
Emergency Swimming Ascent, 134, 139
Entanglement, 84, 134
Entries, 36, 76, 109-110
Environment, 79-91
Equalization, 11, 50
Equipment
    Checklist, 155
    Identification, 26
    Inspection, 108-109
Evaluating Conditions, 107
Exits, 43, 105, 113
Exposure Suits, 19-21

F

Fins, 15-17, 38
First Aid, 131
    Kit, 157
Floats; see Surface Floats
Flying After Diving, 98, 131
Fresh Water Diving, 85

G

Gear
    bag, 25
    inspection, 35, 108-109
Gloves, 21
Goggles, 12

H

Hand Signals, 63-65
Health, 118-119
Hearing, 7
Heat Loss, 7-8, 80
Hood, 21
Hydrotesting, 56
Hyperventilation, 27

I

Immunizations, 118
Information Sources, 167
Instrument Panel, 94

Internal Inspection, 55
Introduction to Diving, 1-2

J

J-Valve; see Valves

K

K-Valve; see Valves
Kit, Spare Parts, 117
Knife, 24

L

Light Rays, 6-7
Logbook, 118
Longshore Current, 88
Low Pressure Inflator, 61
Lung Volume, 9-10, 51, 134, 137

M

Maintenance of Equipment, 19, 22, 44, 54-55, 59
Mask, 12-14
    clearing, 43, 74
    defogging, 33
    squeeze, 41, 50
Mechanics of Pressure, 47
Medical Exam, 118
Metric Conversions, 165-166
Motion, 8
Mouth-to-Mouth Resuscitation, 135, 159

N

Narcosis, 96
Navigation, 112
Negative Buoyancy, 9
Neutral Buoyancy, 9, 18, 23-24, 102-103
No-Decompression Limits, 121-122

O

O-Ring, 68
Oceans, 86-91
Octopus, 61, 138
Open Water
    diving, 106
    diver, 3-4

Opportunities, 147
Overexertion, 28
Overexposure, 7, 80, 85
Overheating, 22
Oxygen, 26-27, 96

P

PADI, 3-4
Panic, 132-133
Plankton Bloom, 80
Plants, 84, 134
Positive Buoyancy, 9, 103
Pregnancy, 119
Pressure, 10-11, 20, 47-51
    relief valve, 18
Problem Recognition, 132
Proficiency Test, 140-141
Purge Valve, 12

Q

Quick Release, 28, 32, 71

R

Recall System, 62
Recompression Chamber, 97
Regulators, 57-58
    clearing, 72-73
Repetitive Diving, 130
Residual Nitrogen, 123
Resource Information, 167
Respiration, 26
Rip Currents, 90

S

Safety Rules, 143-146
Salt Water Diving, 86
Scuba Equipment Assembly, 68-70
Self Rescue, 132
Sinus Squeeze, 49-50
Slate, 63, 117
Smoking, 118
Snorkel, 14-15, 36
    clearing, 36-37
Sound, 7, 62-63
Spare Parts Kit, 117
Squeeze, 49-50

Storing Equipment, 19, 22, 44, 55, 59
Submersible Pressure Gauge, 57, 60, 69, 93
Suiting Up, 30-34, 70-72, 107-108
Sunlight, 7, 85
Surf, 86-90, 113
Surface
    dives, 40-41
    floats, 115
    -supplied, 2
    swimming, 38, 110-111
Swimming, 5, 38, 41

T

Tanks, 52-53, 100-101
    boot, 53
    filling, 54-55, 95
Temperature, 8, 80, 166
Thermocline, 80
Thermometer, 93
Tides, 91

U

Unconscious Diver, 134-135
Undertow, 88
Underwater
    emergencies, 133-134
    light, 117
    slate, 63, 117
    swimming, 41-42
Upwelling, 90-91

V

Valves, 53-55
Visibility, 80-81
Vision, 6-7

W

Watch, Diving, 92
Water
    density, 82
    pressure, 47-48
Watermanship, 5
Waves, 86-89
Weight Belt, 23-24, 30, 99-100
Wet Suits; see Exposure Suits
Women Divers, 119